HAVE YOU
ANYTHING TO DECLARE?

HAVE YOU ANYTHING TO DECLARE?

A Note Book with Commentaries

BY

MAURICE BARING

WILLIAM HEINEMANN LTD
MELBOURNE :: LONDON :: TORONTO

FIRST PUBLISHED 1936
REPRINTED 1936, 1937, 1950
1951

PRINTED IN GREAT BRITAIN
AT THE WINDMILL PRESS
KINGSWOOD, SURREY

DEDICATED TO

NATHALIE

PREFACE

This book is not meant for scholars nor for the learned, but for those who, like myself, although they have only a smattering of letters, are fond of books and fond of reading.

My grateful thanks are due to the following for their kind permission to print passages in prose and verse:

Messrs Seeley and Service for three passages from *Stories from Homer*, by A. J. Church; Mr Leo Myers, for permission to quote from his father's *Essays*; to Mr Belloc, for a sonnet, and some prose; to Messrs Duckworth, for permission to print the same sonnet; to Messrs Methuen, for one of the pieces of prose; to Mr E. V. Lucas, for prose; to Mr H. Salt, for his translation of Lucretius, and to Messrs Watts (who published it); to Messrs John Murray, for several quotations from Robert Browning; to Messrs Macmillan, for some prose from Henry James's novels and some stanzas from Tennyson, and also for a passage from Chesterton's monograph on Browning; to Ernest Benn, Ltd., for some extracts from John Oliver Hobbes's novels, and a poem; to Messrs Hodder and Stoughton, and to Messrs Dodd and Mead, for sentences from G. K. Chesterton's book on Stevenson; to Messrs Chatto and Windus for an excerpt from Stevenson's *Prince Otto*; and two passages from W. H. Mallock's *Is Life Worth Living?*; to Messrs Jonathan Cape, for Professor Chambers's *Life of Sir Thomas More*; to Messrs Allen and Unwin, the publishers of the only authorized edition of Ruskin's works, for a passage from *A Joy for Ever*; to Father Vincent McNabb for some thoughts from his sermons; to Father C. C. Martindale for a sentence from the *Life of St Aloysius*; to Messrs

Heinemann for prose and verse from Swinburne and Stevenson, and the Loeb edition of the classics; to Messrs Longmans Green, for a poem by Andrew Lang and some lines of prose; to MM. Calmann-Lévy for some passages from Renan; to M. Paul Géraldy for an unpublished sentence; to M. Jacques Chardonne and M. André Maurois for sentences; to Miss Elizabeth Belloc for two poems; to Miss Shaw-Stewart for a poem by the late Patrick Shaw-Stewart; and to Mr Marsh, for translations of fragments of La Fontaine as well as for his invaluable help in correcting the proofs.

M.B.

ROTTINGDEAN
November 1936

HAVE YOU
ANYTHING TO DECLARE?

A*

HAVE YOU ANYTHING
TO DECLARE?

I dreamed once that, like Clarence, I had "pass'd the melancholy flood, with that grim Ferryman that poets write of", and that, when we reached the other side, there was a Customs House and an official who had inscribed in golden letters on his cap *Chemins de fer de l'Enfer*, who said to me, "Have you anything to declare?" And he handed me a printed list on which, instead of wine, spirits, tobacco, silk, lace, etc., there was printed Sanskrit, Hebrew, Greek, Latin, French, Italian, German, Spanish, Scandinavian, Chinese, Arabic and Persian, and it was explained to me that this list referred to the literary baggage I had travelled with during my life, and that I need only declare those things of which I had a permanent record either in my memory or in written notebooks. There, sure enough, on the counter before me appeared two boxes, one labelled *Memory*, the other *Notes*. The Customs House official gave me a look, and said: "Small Latin and less Greek?"

And then I woke up.

My dream faded, but the desire to make a declaration of such luggage as I have travelled with and kept, or discarded, remains. I have always enjoyed reading every kind of adventure that others have met with in the kingdom of books, and it is possible that the Customs House declaration of the literary baggage that accompanied me during my life may be of some interest or amusement to my fellow-travellers, and give them the opportunity of comparing notes.

I am making this declaration of literary odds and ends as they come in my notebooks or in my memory. I am not making an anthology, nor choosing what I think best, and arranging it in the order I think best; I am taking my notes as they come, and interrupting what is noted by what I remember, or by what the notes may suggest.

The first question put to me by Charon's prescient Customs House officer was, as I have said, "Small Latin and less Greek?"

If Shakespeare had little Greek, I have less; for I maintain that men who in Shakespeare's day had a smattering of Greek had more Greek than the man who has a smattering of Greek in our day. There was more Greek in the air. And the culture imbibed from the air is the best culture. "Greek, Sir," said Dr Johnson, "is like lace; every man gets as much of it as he can." And on another occasion he said: "Any man who wears a sword and a powdered wig is ashamed to be illiterate." Now it is the other way round; people are ashamed to be literate. But to go back to my Customs House declaration.

I have some scraps of Homer to declare. I will produce them from my portmanteaux of Notes and Memory in the order in which they come, irrespective of what they are about. The *Odyssey* comes before the *Iliad*, because I read it first and Church's *Stories from Homer* before either.

τὴν γὰρ ἀοιδὴν μᾶλλον ἐπικλείουσ' ἄνθρωποι,
ἥ τις ἀκουόντεσσι νεωτάτη ἀμφιπέληται.

Odyssey, Book I, lines 351–352.

For men praise more readily that song which is newest
to their ears.*

Homer and Dante both comment on the swift revolutions
of fashion and taste in matters of literature and art, and note
how men prefer the new to the old; and Dante vehemently
comments on the mutability of mortal achievements:

> *Credette Cimabue nella pintura*
>   *tener lo campo, ed ora ha Giotto il grido....*
>
> . . . .
>
> *Non è 'l mondan romore altro ch' un fiato*
>   *di vento, ch' or vien quinci ed or vien quindi,*
>   *e muta nome perchè muta lato....*

Purgatorio, Canto 11.

For Cimabue deem'd himself secure,
Within the field of painting; Giotto now
Hath caused the former fame to be obscure.

. . . .

The splendours that belong
Unto the fame of earth are but a wind,
That in the same direction lasts not long.

Mrs Ramsay.

Lord Beaconsfield commented on the same fact more lightly:
"Anybody", he said, "amuses me for once. A new acquaintance is like a new book. I prefer it, even if bad, to a classic."

* Where no author's name is given, the translations have been made
by myself.

[3]

ἔνθα δ' ἔπειτα κατέκταθεν, ὅσσοι ἄριστοι.

Odyssey, Book III, line 108.

There and then our best men were killed.

This note is struck by Homer over and over again, but more often and more solemnly in the *Iliad* than in the *Odyssey*.

Homer praises happy marriage.

οὐ μὲν γὰρ τοῦ γε κρεῖσσον καὶ ἄρειον,
ἢ ὅθ᾽ ὁμοφρονέοντε νοήμασιν οἶκον ἔχητον
ἀνὴρ ἠδὲ γυνή· πόλλ᾽ ἄλγεα δυσμενέεσσιν,
χάρματα δ᾽ εὐμενέτῃσι, μάλιστα δέ τ᾽ ἔκλυον αὐτοί.

Odyssey, Book VI, lines 182–185.

For nothing is greater or better than this, when man and wife dwell in the house in harmony, a great grief to their foes, and a joy to their friends, but they know this best themselves.

How different from the sentiments on marriage expressed by young intellectual Communists.

κῆρυξ δ᾽ ἐγγύθεν ἦλθεν ἄγων ἐρίηρον ἀοιδόν,
τὸν πέρι μοῦσα φίλησε, δίδου δ᾽ ἀγαθόν τε κακόν τε·
ὀφθαλμῶν μὲν ἄμερσε, δίδου δ᾽ ἡδεῖαν ἀοιδήν.

Odyssey, Book VIII, lines 62–64.

Then came the herald, leading the good minstrel, whom
the Muse loved above all men, and to whom she gave
both good and evil; she deprived him of sight, but gave
him the gift of sweet song.

Homer wrote his own autobiography and Milton's in these
lines; and if for "sight" you read "hearing", Beethoven's too.

αὐτὰρ ἐμοί γε κατεκλάσθη φίλον ἦτορ·
κλαῖον δ' ἐν λεχέεσσι καθήμενος, οὐδέ νύ μοι κῆρ
ἤθελ' ἔτι ζώειν καὶ ὁρᾶν φάος ἠελίοιο.

Odyssey, Book X, lines 496–498.

My spirit was broken, and I wept as I sat on the bed,
nor had I any longer desire to live, and behold the light
of the sun.

So the Harper in *Wilhelm Meister* when he sang:

Wer nie sein Brod mit Thränen ass,
Wer nie die kummervollen Nächte
Auf seinem Bette weinend sass,
Der kennt euch nicht, ihr himmlischen Mächte.

Who never ate his bread with sorrow,
Who never spent the midnight hours
Weeping and waiting for the morrow—
He knows you not, ye heavenly powers.

Carlyle.

Ἐλπήνωρ δέ τις ἔσκε νεώτατος, οὔτε τι λίην
ἄλκιμος ἐν πολέμῳ οὔτε φρεσὶν ᾗσιν ἀρηρώς·
ὅς μοι ἄνευθ' ἑτάρων ἱεροῖς ἐν δώμασι Κίρκης,
ψύχεος ἱμείρων, κατελέξατο οἰνοβαρείων.
κινυμένων δ' ἑτάρων ὅμαδον καὶ δοῦπον ἀκούσας
ἐξαπίνης ἀνόρουσε καὶ ἐκλάθετο φρεσὶν ᾗσιν
ἄψορρον καταβῆναι ἰὼν ἐς κλίμακα μακρήν,
ἀλλὰ καταντικρὺ τέγεος πέσεν· ἐκ δέ οἱ αὐχὴν
ἀστραγάλων ἐάγη, ψυχὴ δ' Ἀϊδόσδε κατῆλθεν.

Odyssey, Book X, lines 552–560.

It chanced that one Elpenor the youngest, neither over-brave in war, nor excelling in wisdom, was sleeping on the roof in the sacred house of Circe, for the coolness, being heavy with wine. And when he heard the stir of his comrades, he rose up, nor thought him of the ladder, but fell from the roof and broke his neck. And his spirit went down to the house of Hades.

A. J. Church, *Stories from Homer*.

In these nine lines Homer writes a great many long modern novels about young failures and ne'er-do-weel's. Yet Homer tells us all that is necessary: all the elements of the tragedy. When Ulysses leaves Circe's island and seeks the region of the dead, the first Shade he encounters is that of Elpenor, who says to him:

ἆσέ με δαίμονος αἶσα κακὴ καὶ ἀθέσφατος οἶνος.

Odyssey, Book XI, line 61.

An evil doom of some god was my undoing, and measureless wine.

Coppeau, the hero of Zola's novel, *L'Assommoir*, might have said just the same.

"I know", Elpenor says to Ulysses, "that as thou goest hence, thou wilt touch at the Aeaean Isle. There remember me. Leave me not behind unwept and unburied. But burn me with all my armour and make a mound for me on the shore of the grey sea in memory of an unhappy man, that men may yet learn of me."

And Ulysses promised to carry out the wishes of Elpenor

[8]

and he fulfilled his promise as soon as he touched once more at Circe's island.

And thus ends the story that contains the kernel of so many other stories of failures who died young, and of so many novels in English, French and Russian, as long as Stendhal's *Le Rouge et le Noir* and as short as *The Unbearable Bassington* by Saki or *A Handful of Dust* by Evelyn Waugh.

σοὶ δ' ἔπι μὲν μορφὴ ἐπέων, ἔνι δὲ φρένες ἐσθλαί.

Odyssey, Book XI, line 367.

But upon thee is grace of words, and within thee is a heart of wisdom.

A. T. Murray.

T. E. Lawrence translates it:

In your words is a formal beauty to match the graceful order of your ideas,

and Pope translates it:

Wise is thy voice, and noble is thy heart.

The words are spoken by King Alcinous to Ulysses, who has been telling his adventures, and the King is assuring Ulysses that he in no way suspects him of being a liar or an impostor.

ὃς πρὶν μὲν μάλα πολλὰ πάθ᾽ ἄλγεα ὃν κατὰ θυμόν,
ἀνδρῶν τε πτολέμους ἀλεγεινά τε κύματα πείρων·
δὴ τότε γ᾽ ἀτρέμας εὗδε, λελασμένος ὅσσ᾽ ἐπεπόνθει.

Odyssey, Book XIII, lines 90–92.

One who in the past had suffered much in the wars and
from the waves; now he slept at peace forgetful of what
he had suffered.

ὣς ὁ μὲν ἔνθ᾽ ἀπόλωλε, φίλοισι δὲ κήδε᾽ ὀπίσσω
πᾶσιν, ἐμοὶ δὲ μάλιστα, τετεύχαται.

Odyssey, Book XIV, lines 137–138.

Thus has he fallen yonder, and to his friends grief is
allotted for the future, to all, but most of all to me.

χρὴ ξεῖνον παρεόντα φιλεῖν, ἐθέλοντα δὲ πέμπειν.

Odyssey, Book XV, line 74.

Translated by Pope:

Welcome the coming, speed the parting guest.

This was used as a quotation by the ancients, as well as by the modern world. Perhaps Shakespeare caught its echo when he wrote in *Troilus and Cressida*:

For time is like a fashionable host
That slightly shakes his parting guest by th' hand,
And with his arms outstretch'd, as he would fly,
Grasps in the comer; welcome ever smiles
And farewell goes out sighing.

τὴν δ᾽ ἅμα χάρμα καὶ ἄλγος ἕλε φρένα, τὼ δέ οἱ ὄσσε
δακρυόφιν πλῆσθεν, θαλερὴ δέ οἱ ἔσχετο φωνή.

Odyssey, Book XIX, lines 471–472.

Then to her soul joy and grief came in one moment, and
both her eyes were filled with tears, and her speech was
checked.

This refers to Euryclea, the nurse of Ulysses. Ulysses when
he comes has planned not to reveal himself until he is ready to
take vengeance on the suitors who are living in his house. So
he pretends to be a native of Crete, a friend of Ulysses, and
neither his wife nor his old nurse recognizes him, until Euryclea,
when she is washing his feet, knows by the touch the scar left
by a wound he had got long ago hunting a wild boar with the
sons of Autolycus; and so moved is she that she lets fall his
foot into the brazen bowl. And the vessel rings and tilts over,
and the water is spilt on the ground. It was then that with joy
and tears she said: "Thou art in truth Ulysses my dear child,
and I knew thee not until I had touched the body of my lord."

That finishes the *Odyssey*. I come to the *Iliad*.

If one reads the *Iliad* immediately after reading the *Odyssey*, one is at once conscious of a change of atmosphere; one has left the realm of romance and entered that of tragedy.

κάρτιστοι μὲν ἔσαν καὶ καρτίστοις ἐμάχοντο.

Iliad, Book I, lines 267.

The mightiest were these, and with the mightiest they fought.

That is the theme of the *Iliad*. It is the mightiest story of the mightiest men. It is the story of all wars. It is also the greatest dirge for the brave who were doomed to die young, and the sentiments and thoughts which such glorious deeds and events evoke are expressed with a majesty and simplicity which have no parallel in any of the literatures of the world.

"No words that men can any more set side by side", writes Frederick Myers in his *Classical Essays*, "can ever affect the mind again like some of the great passages of Homer. For in them it seems as if all that makes life precious were in the act of being created at once and together—language itself, and the first emotions, and the inconceivable charm of song. When we hear one single sentence of Anticleia's answer, as she begins—

οὔτ᾽ ἐμέ γ᾽ ἐν μεγάροισιν ἐύσκοπος ἰοχέαιρα*—

what words can express the sense which we receive of an effortless and absolute sublimity, the feeling of morning freshness and elemental power, the delight which is to all other intellectual delights what youth is to all other joys? And what a language! which has written, as it were, of itself, those two last words for the poet, which offers them as the fruit of its inmost structure and the bloom of its early day! Beside speech like this, Virgil's seems elaborate, and Dante's crabbed, and Shakespeare's barbarous. There never has been, there never will be, a language like the dead Greek. For Greek had all the merits of other tongues without their accompanying defects. It had the monu-

---

* *Odyssey*, Book XI, line 198: "Neither did the keen-sighted archer-goddess assail me in my halls."

mental weight and brevity of the Latin, without its rigid unmanageability; the copiousness and flexibility of the German without its heavy commonness and guttural superfluity; the pellucidity of the French without its jejuneness; the force and reality of the English without its structureless comminution."

Michael Lomonosov, who lived in the eighteenth century (1714–1765), an historian and in addition a geologist, a grammarian and a poet, and if not the father, at any rate the Peter the Great of the Russian language, said that Russian possessed "the vivacity of French, the strength of German, the softness of Italian, the richness and powerful concision of Greek and Latin".

There is nothing more moving in literature than the speeches of Thetis to Achilles her son; she knowing what his doom is to be:

νῦν δ’ ἅμα τ’ ὠκύμορος καὶ ὀιζυρὸς περὶ πάντων
ἔπλεο.

Iliad, Book I, lines 417–418.

But now art thou doomed both to a swift end and to sorrow above all men.

Then we have the note of lament for those who not only fall in battle, but perish far away from their homes:

ἐν Τροίῃ ἀπόλοντο, φίλης ἀπὸ πατρίδος αἴης.

Iliad, Book II, line 162.

They perished in Troy far away from their dear native land.

To the Greeks there was no prospect of drinking mead in the halls of a sunlit Valhalla, nor of moving, a star among the starry circles of Paradise. Achilles said he would rather be a live dog on earth than King of all the Ghosts in the cold shadowland.

The Trojan ground was as symbolic to the Greeks as the mud of Flanders is to us, where for three centuries Englishmen have fought and died. The line I have just quoted seems to sum the matter up more tersely, simply and beautifully than any others. The beautiful lines of Quevedo:

Su tumba son de Flándes las campañas
Y su epitafio la sangrienta luna,

The fields of Flanders are his sepulchre
And the moon shot with blood, his epitaph,

have a special message for many English men and women, but Homer conveys more with fewer words and without the aid of an image.

Homer strikes another equally sad chord a little later on those who lie buried at home:

τοὺς δ' ἤδη κάτεχεν φυσίζοος αἶα
ἐν Λακεδαίμονι αὖθι, φίλῃ ἐν πατρίδι γαίῃ.

Iliad, Book III, lines 243–244.

For they already were held fast in the life-giving earth, far away in Lacedaemon, their dear native land.

[18]

αὖτις ἐπεσσεύοντο νεῶν ἄπο καὶ κλισιάων
ἠχῇ, ὡς ὅτε κῦμα πολυφλοίσβοιο θαλάσσης
αἰγιαλῷ μεγάλῳ βρέμεται, σμαραγεῖ δέ τε πόντος.

Iliad, Book II, lines 208–210.

And they hastened back to the place of assembly from their ships with a noise as when a wave of the loud-sounding sea thunders on the long beach, and the ocean roars.

Andrew Lang wrote:

> The surge and thunder of the Odyssey.

That of the *Iliad* is even more tremendous, and these three lines are a good example of it.

ἄλλος δ' ἄλλῳ ἔρεζε θεῶν αἰειγενετάων,
εὐχόμενος θάνατόν τε φυγεῖν καὶ μῶλον Ἄρηος.

Iliad, Book II, lines 400–401.

And they made sacrifice to the eternal gods and prayed
that they might escape from death and the evil of war.

Homer never thought of war except as an unmixed evil. There
was only one thing that made the Trojan war worth while to the
combatants, and that was the beauty of Helen. When they
beheld Helen, all the rest was forgotten:

οἱ δ' ὡς οὖν εἶδονθ' Ἑλένην ἐπὶ πύργον ἰοῦσαν,
ἦκα πρὸς ἀλλήλους ἔπεα πτερόεντ' ἀγόρευον·
"οὐ νέμεσις Τρῶας καὶ ἐυκνήμιδας Ἀχαιοὺς
τοιῇδ' ἀμφὶ γυναικὶ πολὺν χρόνον ἄλγεα πάσχειν·
αἰνῶς ἀθανάτῃσι θεῇς εἰς ὦπα ἔοικεν."

Iliad, Book III, lines 154–158.

And when they saw Helen coming along the wall, they
whispered softly among themselves: "Small wonder that
Trojans and the well-greaved Achaeans should suffer
greatly and long for such a woman, for she is marvellously
like to the immortal goddesses to look upon."

That is the best description of female beauty in literature.
Homer gives no catalogue of Helen's charms, nor describes
her features, nor gives any details. A description of that kind
never leaves the reader with a definite impression. He simply
says she is like a goddess, and tells us the effect her beauty had
upon those who beheld her. The result is that we see her walking
on the walls of Troy, and understand why the Greeks and
Trojans sometimes thought the long war was worth while.

Pope's *Iliad* has generally been found fault with for not being
like Homer. "A very pretty poem, Mr Pope; but you must not
call it Homer." Few people at the present day realize what a
magnificent poem it is. Pope's couplet, the particular bow he
used, is as difficult to wield as that of Ulysses. "Homer's Homer
is the best," wrote Augustine Birrell, "but Pope's is the second

best, and the others are a matter of controversy." Here are a few lines taken at random from my notebook:

> A faithful servant to a foreign lord,
> In peace, in war, for ever at his side,
> Near his lov'd master, as he liv'd, he dy'd.
>
> *Iliad*, Book XV, lines 503–505.

> In youth's first bloom reluctantly he dies.
>
> *Iliad*, Book XV, line 529.

> Yet Jove deferr'd the death he was to pay,
> And gave what fate allow'd, the honours of a day!
>
> *Iliad*, Book XV, lines 738–739.

> That worst of tyrants, an usurping crowd.
>
> *Iliad*, Book II, line 242.

> Ye gods, what dastards would our host command?
> Swept to the war, the lumber of a land.
>
> *Iliad*, Book II, lines 239–240.

> Dim thro' th' eclipse of fate, the rays divine
> Of sovereign state with faded splendor shine.
>
> *Odyssey*, Book XX, lines 243–244.

> As when some heav'n-taught Poet charms the ear
> (Suspending sorrow with celestial strain
> Breathed from the gods to soften human pain),
> Time steals away with unregarded wing,
> And the soul hears him, tho' he cease to sing.
>
> *Odyssey*, Book XVII, lines 609–613.

All this seems to me very good verse. Pope is an interesting example of how the whirligig of Time affects a very great reputation. Critics of his day, Dr Johnson for instance, thought that Pope was a matchless poet, and that hundreds of years would elapse before the world would see such another. Then came the romantic movement, and in its first flush the romantic writers still admired Pope; Byron looked upon his work as something beyond his reach, and compared it to a Greek temple, thereby afterwards eliciting the scorn of Matthew Arnold. Then, as time went on, the Victorian critics looked down upon Pope;

[21]

his work was thought to be an elegant effort in confectionery: a wedding cake. Then came the war, and the breaking of the Victorian ideals, idols, and especially the Victorian critics; Lytton Strachey and Edith Sitwell sang once more the praises of Pope, but no young man appeared who could bend his bow nor emulate the wit, the fire, and the sound of his golden couplets. They cannot even parody Pope. The heroic couplet is an instrument which no one of the present day can use. It is an instrument which no one has played since Byron and Crabbe.

οἵη περ φύλλων γενεή, τοίη δὲ καὶ ἀνδρῶν.
φύλλα τὰ μέν τ᾿ ἄνεμος χαμάδις χέει, ἄλλα δέ θ᾿ ὕλη
τηλεθόωσα φύει, ἔαρος δ᾿ ἐπιγίγνεται ὥρῃ·
ὣς ἀνδρῶν γενεὴ ἡ μὲν φύει, ἡ δ᾿ ἀπολήγει.

Iliad, Book VI, lines 146–149.

Even as the generations of leaves, so are also those of men.
As for the leaves, the wind scatters some upon the earth,
but the forest as it buds brings forth new leaves when the
spring is come: even so one generation of men arises and
another passes away.

There is no melancholy deeper or more dignified than Homer's,
when he writes such lines as these.

Here is an example of the infinite tenderness of his pictures of womanhood and children:

ἥ οἱ ἔπειτ᾽ ἤντησ᾽, ἅμα δ᾽ ἀμφίπολος κίεν αὐτῇ
παῖδ᾽ ἐπὶ κόλπῳ ἔχουσ᾽ ἀταλάφρονα, νήπιον αὔτως,
Ἑκτορίδην ἀγαπητόν, ἀλίγκιον ἀστέρι καλῷ.

Iliad, Book VI, lines 399–401.

She now met him, and with her came a handmaid bearing in her bosom a tender boy, a baby, the well-beloved son of Hector, like a beautiful star.

Here is another phrase spoken by Andromache and laden with intolerable pathos:

ἐμοὶ δέ κε κέρδιον εἴη
σεῦ ἀφαμαρτούσῃ χθόνα δύμεναι· οὐ γὰρ ἔτ' ἄλλη
ἔσται θαλπωρή, ἐπεὶ ἂν σύ γε πότμον ἐπίσπῃς.

Iliad, Book VI, lines 410–412.

For me it would be better to go down to the grave if I lose thee, for nevermore shall any comfort be mine when thou hast met thy fate.

And here a line of ineffable peace:

νὺξ δ' ἤδη τελέθει· ἀγαθὸν καὶ νυκτὶ πιθέσθαι.

Iliad, Book VII, line 282.

For the night is already at hand, and it is well to yield to the night.

This reminds me of the last sentence of Turgenev's novel, *Fathers and Sons*:

But the heat of the noontide wanes, and evening comes and night, and there is a return into a tranquil refuge, where sweet slumber awaits the weary and the afflicted.

Both these passages make me think of Beethoven, who among musicians easily achieves the tragedy and the final peace of Homer.

μήκων δ' ὡς ἑτέρωσε κάρη βάλεν, ᾗ τ' ἐνὶ κήπῳ,
καρπῷ βριθομένη νοτίῃσί τε εἰαρινῇσιν·
ὡς ἑτέρωσ' ἤμυσε κάρη πήληκι βαρυνθέν.

Iliad, Book VIII, lines 306–308.

And he bowed his head to one side, like a poppy that in
the garden is laden with its fruit and the rain of spring,
so bowed he to one side his head laden with his helmet.

This is the first picture in a classic family of bended and
broken blossoms.

Here is Sappho's:

οἴαν τὰν ὑάκινθον ἐν οὔρεσι ποίμενες ἄνδρες
πόσσι καταστείβουσι, χάμαι δ' ἐπιπορφύρει ἄνθος.

Like the hyacinth which the shepherds tread under foot
upon the mountains, and its flower lies purple on the
ground.

Then Virgil's:

> Purpureus veluti cum flos succisus aratro
> languescit moriens lassove papavera collo
> demisere caput, pluvia cum forte gravantur.

Aeneid, Book IX, lines 435–437.

Instead of translating these lines I will quote a parallel from
Matthew Arnold's *Sohrab and Rustum*:

> And he saw that Youth,
> Of age and looks to be his own dear son,
> Piteous and lovely, lying on the sand,
> Like some rich hyacinth, which by the scythe
> Of an unskilful gardener has been cut,
> Mowing the garden grass-plots near its bed,
> And lies, a fragrant tower of purple bloom,
> On the mown, dying grass.

But both these passages are excelled by the closer terseness,
the stricter economy and more magical melody of Catullus:

> Velut prati
> ultimi flos, praetereunte postquam
> tactus aratro est.

These lines used to come into my head whenever I saw Sarah Bernhardt in the last act of *Phèdre*, when, having taken poison, she tottered on to the stage, leaning on her attendants, and her voice, half dead and already faint and chill with the air of Limbo, breathed the words:

> J'ai voulu devant vous exposant mes remords,
> Par un chemin plus lent descendre chez les morts.

Anatole France points out the subtle music of this second line by saying: "You have only to change one word and for 'lent' read 'long' to ruin its whole beauty and deprive it of its magic." The speech goes on:

> J'ai pris, j'ai fait couler dans mes brûlantes veines
> Un poison que Médée apporta dans Athènes.
> Déjà jusqu'à mon cœur le venin parvenu
> Dans ce cœur expirant jette un froid inconnu.
> Déjà je ne vois plus qu'à travers un nuage,
> Et le ciel, et l'époux que ma présence outrage;
> Et la mort à mes yeux dérobant la clarté
> Rend au jour qu'ils souillaient toute sa pureté.

As Sarah Bernhardt spoke the last two lines, her head dropped on her shoulder, just as Catullus describes the flower, or Michael Field in this poem (about a Camellia):

> And one of them—how lovely in her mode!—
> One of them had the magic power to die;
> Slid from the stem where she abode
> With mournful violence: her petals lie
> Broke on the sudden from their mass, and all
> The action stately as a funeral.

οἷος δ’ ἐκ νεφέων ἀναφαίνεται οὔλιος ἀστὴρ
παμφαίνων, τοτὲ δ’ αὗτις ἔδυ νέφεα σκιόεντα,
ὣς Ἕκτωρ ὁτὲ μέν τε μετὰ πρώτοισι φάνεσκεν,
ἄλλοτε δ’ ἐν πυμάτοισι κελεύων.

Iliad, Book XI, lines 64–67.

Even as from the clouds a disastrous star gleams, and glitters, and sinks again behind the shadowy clouds, so would Hector appear now among the foremost and now among the hindmost giving orders.

The glory of the young in Homer, the might of Achilles, the nobility of Hector, is the silver glory of a nimbus; there is a shadow of doom about them. When Aeneas beholds the shade of Marcellus:

Videbat
Egregium forma juvenem et fulgentibus armis,

A youth of surpassing beauty and flashing arms,
Virgil adds:

Sed nox atra caput tristi circumvolat umbra,

But black night with mortal shadow hangs about his head.

καὶ τότ' Ἀπόλλωνα προσέφη νεφεληγερέτα Ζεύς·
"εἰ δ' ἄγε νῦν, φίλε Φοῖβε, κελαινεφὲς αἷμα κάθηρον
ἐλθὼν ἐκ βελέων Σαρπηδόνα, καί μιν ἔπειτα
πολλὸν ἀποπρὸ φέρων λοῦσον ποταμοῖο ῥοῇσιν
χρῖσόν τ' ἀμβροσίῃ, περὶ δ' ἄμβροτα εἵματα ἕσσον·
πέμπε δέ μιν πομποῖσιν ἅμα κραιπνοῖσι φέρεσθαι,
Ὕπνῳ καὶ Θανάτῳ διδυμάοσιν, οἵ ῥά μιν ὦκα
θήσουσ' ἐν Λυκίης εὐρείης πίονι δήμῳ,
ἔνθα ἑ ταρχύσουσι κασίγνητοί τε ἔται τε
τύμβῳ τε στήλῃ τε· τὸ γὰρ γέρας ἐστὶ θανόντων."
ὣς ἔφατ', οὐδ' ἄρα πατρὸς ἀνηκούστησεν Ἀπόλλων.
βῆ δὲ κατ' Ἰδαίων ὀρέων ἐς φύλοπιν αἰνήν,
αὐτίκα δ' ἐκ βελέων Σαρπηδόνα δῖον ἀείρας,
πολλὸν ἀποπρὸ φέρων λοῦσεν ποταμοῖο ῥοῇσιν
χρῖσέν τ' ἀμβροσίῃ, περὶ δ' ἄμβροτα εἵματα ἕσσεν·
πέμπε δέ μιν πομποῖσιν ἅμα κραιπνοῖσι φέρεσθαι,
Ὕπνῳ καὶ Θανάτῳ διδυμάοσιν, οἵ ῥά μιν ὦκα
κάτθεσαν ἐν Λυκίης εὐρείης πίονι δήμῳ.

Iliad, Book XVI, lines 666–683.

The Death of Sarpedon

And Zeus the cloud-gatherer then spoke to Apollo, Arise,
Phoebus, arise, and cleanse the dark blood from Sarpedon,
when thou hast taken him out of range of the darts, and
then bear him far away and bathe him in the streams of
the river, and anoint him with ambrosia and clothe him
with immortal vesture, and give him to the swift escort
to bear with them, to the Twin brothers Sleep and Death,
who shall carry him swiftly to the rich land of broad
Lycia; there shall his brother and his kinsmen bury him
with mound and pillar; for that is the due of the dead.
So spake he, and Apollo obeyed his father's command
and he descended from the hills of Ida into the battle.
He lifted the great Sarpedon out of range of the darts,
and when he had borne him away, bathed him in the
streams of the river, and anointed him with ambrosia
and clothed him with immortal vesture, and gave him to
the swift escort to bear with them, to the Twin brothers

Sleep and Death, who speedily laid him in the rich land of broad Lycia.

If the whole *Iliad* had to be destroyed except for one passage, these eighteen lines are those which I would preserve; and if only three lines were to be preserved, I would choose lines 681–683. A. J. Church abridges the passage thus in his *Stories from Homer*:

> And so the battle raged, till no one would have known the great Sarpedon, so covered was he with spears and blood and dust. But at the last the Greeks drove back the men of Troy from the body, and stripped the arms, the body itself they harmed not. For Apollo came down at the bidding of Zeus and carried it out of the midst of the battle, and washed it with water and anointed it with ambrosia, and wrapped it in the garment of the gods. And then he gave it to Sleep and Death, and these two carried it to Lycia, his fatherland.

Here is Belloc's translation of the last three lines:

> And he gave Sarpedon dead to be borne by swift companions, to Death and Sleep, twin brethren, who bore him through the air to Lycia, that broad and pleasant land,

and Pope's of lines 676–683:

> Apollo bows, and from mount Ida's height,
> Swift to the field precipitates his flight;
> Thence from the war the breathless hero bore,
> Veil'd in a cloud, to silver Simois' shore:
> There bath'd his honourable wounds, and drest
> His manly members in th' immortal vest;
> And with perfumes of sweet ambrosial dews,
> Restores his freshness, and his form renews.
> Then Sleep and Death, two twins of winged race,
> Of matchless swiftness, but of silent pace,
> Receiv'd Sarpedon, at the god's command,
> And in a moment reach'd the Lycian Land;

ὁ δ' ἐν στροφάλιγγι κονίης
κεῖτο μέγας μεγαλωστί, λελασμένος ἱπποσυνάων.

Iliad, Book XVI, lines 775–776.

But he in the whirl of dust lay great in his might, forgetful of his horsemanship.

This picture is like a fragment of a Phidian frieze.

οὐ μὲν γάρ τί πού ἐστιν ὀιζυρώτερον ἀνδρὸς
πάντων, ὅσσα τε γαῖαν ἔπι πνείει τε καὶ ἕρπει.

Iliad, Book XVII, lines 446-447.

For there is naught more miserable than man of all
things that breathe and crawl upon the earth.

Homer in his immense sadness does not rail at fate or the
gods, he just states the fact that man is born to misery. He is
sad as Dante, when Dante says:

Giù per lo mondo senza fine amaro.

As sad as Shakespeare, when he says:

Life's but a walking shadow, a poor player
That struts and frets his hour upon the stage
And then is heard no more.

As sad as Beethoven's utterance in the Scherzo in the Fifth
Symphony. But the difference between the sadness of these and
that, for instance, of Leopardi, is that we feel that Homer might
have ended by writing a *Hymn to Joy*, as Beethoven did in the
Ninth Symphony, as Dante did in the *Paradiso*, as Shakespeare
did in *The Tempest*; but one cannot imagine Leopardi writing a
hymn to Joy; and although Homer was without the new
knowledge that Shakespeare, Dante and Leopardi enjoyed,
in his sadness there is no whine.

"Ξάνθε, τί μοι θάνατον μαντεύεαι; οὐδέ τί σε χρή.
εὖ νύ τοι οἶδα καὶ αὐτός, ὅ μοι μόρος ἐνθάδ᾽ ὀλέσθαι,
νόσφι φίλου πατρὸς καὶ μητέρος· ἀλλὰ καὶ ἔμπης
οὐ λήξω πρὶν Τρῶας ἄδην ἐλάσαι πολέμοιο."

Iliad, Book XIX, lines 420–423.

Xanthus, why dost thou foretell my death? Thou hast
no need. I know well of myself that it is my fate to fall
here, far away from my dear father and mother; but
even so I will not cease until I have made the Trojans
weary of battle.

This is what Achilles says to Xanthus, his immortal horse.
Achilles, after the death of Patroclus, is stirred to fight once
more, and puts on the gleaming armour made for him by
Hephaestus; and as he mounts his chariot to go into battle,
cries out to the horses of his father, to Xanthus and Balius, and
bids them bring their charioteer back safely home, and leave
him not there as they did Patroclus. And then "Horse Xanthus",
Homer says, "from beneath the yoke spoke to him, and the
goddess Hera gave him speech: 'Yes, verily, this time we will
save thee, great Achilles, although the day of doom is at hand
for thee, nor shall we be the cause of it, but a mighty god and
insuperable fate.'" And Achilles makes reply in the words I
started by quoting. It is one of the most magnificent passages
in the whole of the *Iliad*; and yet commentators have been found
to dispute its authenticity, on the grounds that there is no other
example in Homer of a horse speaking. But why should there
be? No one else except Achilles had a pair of immortal horses.
And the gods during the course of the Trojan war did many
things more strange and more difficult than to produce a talking
horse.

There are other talking horses in literature. In Grimm's story
The Goose Girl there is a horse called Falada, who not only
talks, but talks after its head has been cut off, and in rhyme.
There is also Anstey's *Talking Horse* whose name was Brutus,
and who was ridden disastrously by Mr Gustavus Pulvertoft.

ἀλλά, φίλος, θάνε καὶ σύ· τίη ὀλοφύρεαι οὕτως;
κάτθανε καὶ Πάτροκλος, ὅ περ σέο πολλὸν ἀμείνων.

Iliad, Book XXI, lines 106–107.

No, friend, die thou also; why shouldst thou lament thus? Patroclus died, a better man than thou.

These are the words which Achilles says to Lycaon, a son of Priam. The story of Lycaon is one of the bitter little incidents that are characteristic of all wars in all times and in all countries. Lycaon had already been made prisoner by Achilles, who had caught him in his father's orchard cutting the shoots of a wild fig tree for the rims of a chariot. Achilles had sold him to the son of Jason, from whom he had been ransomed at a great price, and now he had come back to his father's house and for eleven days had joy among his friends, till on the twelfth day, as he was fleeing unarmed from the river Xanthus, he encountered Achilles. He begged Achilles to spare his life, seeing that he was not sprung from the same womb as Hector, who slew Patroclus. But Achilles "all ungentle" declared to him there was not now one Trojan that should escape death, and he killed Lycaon, and flung him into the river which the gods called Xanthus and men Scamander, to be food for the fishes; "neither" he said "shall thy mother lay thee on the bier and make lament".

νῦν αὖτέ με μοῖρα κιχάνει.
μὴ μὰν ἀσπουδί γε καὶ ἀκλειῶς ἀπολοίμην,
ἀλλὰ μέγα ῥέξας τι καὶ ἐσσομένοισι πυθέσθαι.

Iliad, Book XXII, lines 303–305.

But now the hour of my doom has come. But not without
a struggle let me die, nor inglorious, but after the doing
of a great deed, that men that are yet to be shall tell of.

The words of Hector when, deserted by Deiphobus and cheated
by the goddess Athene, he knows that his end has come.
Church tells it thus:

> Then Hector knew that his end was come, and he said
> to himself, "Now have the gods called me to my doom.
> I thought that Deiphobus was near; but he is within the
> walls, and the help which he promised me was but a cheat
> with which Athene cheated me. Zeus and Apollo are
> with me no more; but, if I must die, let me at least die in
> such a deed as men of after time may hear of."

And immediately after he spoke, he drew his sword and
rushed on the great Achilles. And Achilles charged to meet
him and drove home his spear where by the collar bone the
neck joins the shoulder, and Hector fell in the dust.

> But oh! not lovely Helen, nor the pride
> Of that most ancient Ilium matched with doom.
> Men murdered Priam in his royal room
> And Troy was burned with fire and Hector died.
> For even Hector's dreadful day was more
> Than all his breathing courage dared defend,
> The armouréd light and bulwark of the war
> Trailed his long story to the accustomed end.
>
> He was the city's buttress, Priam's son,
> The soldier born in bivouac praises great
> And horns in double front of battle won,
> Yet down he went: when unremembering fate
> Felled him at last with all his armour on.
> Hector: the Horseman: in the Scæan gate.

Belloc.

οὐ θέμις ἐστὶ λοετρὰ καρήατος ἆσσον ἱκέσθαι,
πρίν γ' ἐνὶ Πάτροκλον θέμεναι πυρὶ σῆμά τε χεῦαι
κείρασθαί τε κόμην, ἐπεὶ οὔ μ' ἔτι δεύτερον ὧδε
ἵξετ' ἄχος κραδίην, ὄφρα ζωοῖσι μετείω.

Iliad, Book XXIII, lines 44–47.

It may not be that water shall touch my head, until I
have laid Patroclus upon the fire and have heaped him
a mound, and cut off my hair, since never again shall a
second grief thus reach my heart so long as I live.

These are the words spoken by Achilles after he had slain
Hector and dragged his corpse round the walls of Troy.

ἤλυθες Οὐλυμπόνδε, θεὰ Θέτι, κηδομένη περ,
πένθος ἄλαστον ἔχουσα μετὰ φρεσίν.

Iliad, Book XXIV, lines 104–105.

Thou art come to Olympus, goddess Thetis, for all thy
sorrow, although thou art comfortless at heart.

The grief of Thetis and the sadness of Achilles were experienced by many during the Great War. There is a moving expression of this sadness in a poem which was found written by himself in a copy of *The Shropshire Lad* belonging to Patrick Shaw-Stewart, who was killed in France in 1917. The poem was written in 1916.

I saw a man this morning
Who did not wish to die;
I ask and cannot answer
If otherwise wish I.

Fair broke the day this morning
Against the Dardanelles;
The breeze blew soft, the morn's cheeks
Were cold as cold sea-shells.

But other shells are waiting
Across the Aegean sea,
Shrapnel and high explosive,
Shells and hells for me.

O hell of ships and cities,
Hell of men like me!
Fatal second Helen,
Why must I follow thee?*

Achilles came to Troyland
And I to Chersonese:
He turned from wrath to battle
And I from three days' peace.

Was it so hard, Achilles,
So very hard to die?
Thou knowest and I know not—
So much the happier I.

I will go back this morning
From Imbros over the sea;
Stand in the trench, Achilles,
Flame-capped, and shout for me.

* I am told he was thinking of a chorus in the *Agamemnon*, in which Aeschylus puns on the name Helen.

[39]

"μνῆσαι πατρὸς σοῖο, θεοῖς ἐπιείκελ' Ἀχιλλεῦ,
τηλίκου ὥς περ ἐγών, ὀλοῷ ἐπὶ γήραος οὐδῷ.
καὶ μέν που κεῖνον περιναιέται ἀμφὶς ἐόντες
τείρουσ', οὐδέ τις ἔστιν ἀρὴν καὶ λοιγὸν ἀμῦναι.
ἀλλ' ἦ τοι κεῖνός γε σέθεν ζώοντος ἀκούων
χαίρει τ' ἐν θυμῷ ἐπί τ' ἔλπεται ἤματα πάντα
ὄψεσθαι φίλον υἱὸν ἀπὸ Τροίηθεν ἰόντα·
αὐτὰρ ἐγὼ πανάποτμος, ἐπεὶ τέκον υἷας ἀρίστους
Τροίῃ ἐν εὐρείῃ, τῶν δ' οὔ τινά φημι λελεῖφθαι.
πεντήκοντά μοι ἦσαν, ὅτ' ἤλυθον υἷες Ἀχαιῶν·
ἐννεακαίδεκα μέν μοι ἰῆς ἐκ νηδύος ἦσαν,
τοὺς δ' ἄλλους μοι ἔτικτον ἐνὶ μεγάροισι γυναῖκες.
τῶν μὲν πολλῶν θοῦρος Ἄρης ὑπὸ γούνατ' ἔλυσεν·
ὃς δέ μοι οἶος ἔην, εἴρυτο δὲ ἄστυ καὶ αὐτούς,
τὸν σὺ πρώην κτεῖνας ἀμυνόμενον περὶ πάτρης,
Ἕκτορα. τοῦ νῦν εἵνεχ' ἱκάνω νῆας Ἀχαιῶν,
λυσόμενος παρὰ σεῖο, φέρω δ' ἀπερείσι' ἄποινα.
ἀλλ' αἰδεῖο θεούς, Ἀχιλεῦ, αὐτόν τ' ἐλέησον
μνησάμενος σοῦ πατρός· ἐγὼ δ' ἐλεεινότερός περ,
ἔτλην δ', οἷ' οὔ πώ τις ἐπιχθόνιος βροτὸς ἄλλος,
ἀνδρὸς παιδοφόνοιο ποτὶ στόμα χεῖρ' ὀρέγεσθαι."
ὣς φάτο, τῷ δ' ἄρα πατρὸς ὑφ' ἵμερον ὦρσε γόοιο·
ἁψάμενος δ' ἄρα χειρὸς ἀπώσατο ἦκα γέροντα.
τὼ δὲ μνησαμένω ὁ μὲν Ἕκτορος ἀνδροφόνοιο
κλαῖ' ἀδινά, προπάροιθε ποδῶν Ἀχιλῆος ἐλυσθείς,
αὐτὰρ Ἀχιλεὺς κλαῖεν ἑὸν πατέρ', ἄλλοτε δ' αὖτε
Πάτροκλον· τῶν δὲ στοναχὴ κατὰ δώματ' ὀρώρει.

Iliad, Book XXIV, lines 486–512.

Priam seeks Achilles in his tent to ransom the body of Hector.

"Remember thy father, godlike Achilles, like myself on the grievous road of old age.

"Most likely those around him are entreating him badly, neither is there anyone to defend him from strife and disaster. But so long as he hears of thee being alive he is glad at heart, and lives in hope every day of seeing his dear son return from Troy. But I, I am all-hapless, for I begat the best sons in the broad land of Troy, and

of them I say not one is left. I had fifty sons when the
sons of the Achæans came; nineteen were born to me of
one mother, and the others of women in the halls of the
palace. Of these Ares had stricken the greater part. And
he who alone was left to me, who guarded city and men,
him thou hast killed now, as he fought for his country:
Hector. For his sake I am now come to the ships of the
Achæans to win him back from thee, and I bear invaluable
ransoms.

"But fear the gods, Achilles, and remembering thy own
father, have pity on me; I am far more miserable than
he, and I have confronted what no other mortal on the
earth hath yet endured, to stretch forth my hand to the
face of him who killed my son."

Thus spake he and in Achilles he aroused desire to weep
for his father; and he took the old man by the hand and
gently put him from him. And they both thought of
their dead and wept: Priam for man-slaying Hector, as he
fell at Achilles' feet, and Achilles wept for his own father,
and for Patroclus, and the house was filled with their
lamentations.

A little later Achilles says to Priam:

καὶ σέ, γέρον, τὸ πρὶν μὲν ἀκούομεν ὄλβιον εἶναι.

Iliad, Book XXIV, line 543.

They say that thou too, old man, once upon a time wast
blest.

In this interview between Priam and Achilles, as it is told by
Homer, Priam says all that can be said about the most tragic
fact inherent in all wars—the irreparable wrong and the
unending, incurable sorrow inflicted on one another by men
who but for the accident of war—that one is on one side and
one is on the other—would feel nothing for one another but
affection and respect.

Mr Britling's experience and the record of it adds nothing to
that of Priam when he sees it through.

Here is an Homeric epigram from the *Margites*:

πόλλ᾽ ἠπίστατο ἔργα κακῶς δ᾽ ἠπίστατο πάντα.
τὸν δ᾽ οὔτ᾽ ἄρ᾽ σκαπτῆρα θεοὶ θέσαν οὔτ᾽ ἀροτῆρα
οὔτ᾽ ἄλλως τι σοφόν, πάσης δ᾽ ἡμάρτανε τέχνης,
Μουσάων θεράπων καὶ ἑκηβόλου Ἀπόλλωνος.

He knew a great many things, but he knew them all badly. The Gods had made him neither a delver, nor a ploughman, nor anything useful; he was master of no trade: a follower of the Muses and of the long-bowed Apollo.

Leconte de Lisle translates the epigram as follows:

Il savait de nombreuses choses, mais il les savait toutes mal. Les Dieux ne l'avaient fait ni jardinier, ni laboureur; il n'était propre à rien, et il n'avait aucun art. Serviteur des Muses et de l'Archer Apollon.

I have no doubt about the elegance of this translation; it is for scholars to pronounce on its accuracy.

Although *art* is no doubt an accurate rendering of τέχνη I should have thought that in this particular case the word *métier* would have been more exact. Because if the subject of the poem in question was the servant of the Muses, and of the long-bowed Apollo, he must have been an artist although he followed no profession. He was, in fact, an amateur. (According to the Oxford text the last line does not belong to the epigram, in which case my argument is nonsense.)

In a story I once wrote called *A Luncheon Party* the following fragment of conversation occurs between Willmott, an actor-manager, and Giles, a critic and man-of-letters. They are discussing Rostand.

Willmott says: "He's an amateur. He's never written professionally for his bread, but only for pleasure."

"But in that sense", said Giles, "God is an amateur."

Giles was drawn from Edmund Gosse.

The next items I have to declare are a few fragments of Euripides. The last lines of the last chorus in the *Medea*:

πολλῶν ταμίας Ζεὺς ἐν Ὀλύμπῳ,
πολλὰ δ' ἀέλπτως κραίνουσι θεοί·
καὶ τὰ δοκηθέντ' οὐκ ἐτελέσθη,
τῶν δ' ἀδοκήτων πόρον ηὗρε θεός.
τοιόνδ' ἀπέβη τόδε πρᾶγμα.

Zeus in Olympus disposes of many things; what the gods ordain, no man foresaw. What we looked for is not fulfilled: the gods bring unlooked-for things to pass. Thus befell this strange event.

δυσέρωτες δὴ φαινόμεθ' ὄντες
τοῦδ', ὅτι τοῦτο στίλβει κατὰ γῆν
δι' ἀπειροσύνην ἄλλου βιότου
κοὐκ ἀπόδειξιν τῶν ὑπὸ γαίας·
μύθοις δ' ἄλλως φερόμεσθα.

Hippolytus, lines 193–197.

We cling—this earth's poor sunshine-gleam:
 Naught know we of the life to come,
 There speak no voices from the tomb:
We drift on Fable's shadowy stream.

Arthur Way.

This chorus-ending from the *Hippolytus* which closes on the dominant, wistfully, perhaps was in Browning's mind when he wrote:

A chorus-ending from Euripides.

δεινὰ γὰρ παντᾷ ποτιπνεῖ, μέλισσα
δ' οἷα τις πεπόταται.

Hippolytus, lines 563-564.

The dread one breathes upon all life, winging her flight
like a bee.

A chorus-ending.

Another perfect illustration of Browning's line.

πότνια, πότνια νύξ,
ὑπνοδότειρα τῶν πολυπόνων βροτῶν,
ἐρεβόθεν ἴθι, μόλε μόλε κατάπτερος
τὸν Ἀγαμεμνόνιον ἐπὶ δόμον.

Orestes, lines 175–178.

This was translated for me by the late Hugh Macnaghten,
Vice-Provost of Eton:

> Come, holy holy night,
> Giver of sleep to man in care's despite,
> Rise from the dark strong-winged, and hither come
> To Agamemnon's home.

Longfellow wrote a beautiful equivalent to it:

> Peace! Peace! Orestes-like I breathe this prayer!
> Descend with broad-winged flight,
> The welcome, the thrice-prayed for, the most fair,
> The best-beloved Night!

Some fragments of Sophocles:

ὁρῶ γὰρ ἡμᾶς οὐδὲν ὄντας ἄλλο πλὴν
εἴδωλ᾽ ὅσοιπερ ζῶμεν ἢ κούφην σκιάν.

Ajax, lines 125–126.

Alas! What are mortals but phantoms and unsubstantial shadows?

ἐγὼ γὰρ ἤμην ἐκπεπληγμένη φόβῳ
μή μοι τὸ κάλλος ἄλγος ἐξεύροι ποτέ.

Trachiniae, ines 24–25.

For me, I sat distracted by the dread
That beauty in the end might prove my bane.

Storr.

Beauty has almost always proved the bane of the very beautiful.

τότ' ἄν τις εἰσίδοιτο, τὴν αὐτοῦ σκοπῶν
πρᾶξιν, κακοῖσιν οἷς ἐγὼ βαρύνομαι.

Trachiniae, lines 151–152.

Only the woman who knows the cares of wedlock by experience knows what I endure.

Any wife to any husband.

χοὖτος τεθνηκὼς ἦν· λόγῳ δέ σ' ἐν βραχεῖ
τοῦτ' ἐκδιδάξω· πόλεμος οὐδέν' ἄνδρ' ἑκὼν
αἱρεῖ πονηρόν, ἀλλὰ τοὺς χρηστοὺς ἀεί.

Philoctetes, lines 435–437.

Dead like the rest, for this is true: war never chooses an
evil man, but the good.

οὐ δῆτ’, ἐπεί τοι τὴν μὲν αὐτίχ’ ἡμέραν,
ὁπηνίκ’ ἔζει θυμός, ἥδιστον δέ μοι
τὸ κατθανεῖν ἦν καὶ τὸ λευσθῆναι πέτροις,
οὐδεὶς ἔρωτ’ ἐς τόνδ’ ἐφαίνετ’ ὠφελῶν.

Oedipus at Colonus, lines 433–436.

Not so; for mark you, on that very day
When in the tempest of my soul I prayed
Death, even death by stoning, none appeared
To further that wild longing.

Storr.

Ἔρωτι μέν νυν ὅστις ἀντανίσταται
πύκτης ὅπως ἐς χεῖρας οὐ καλῶς φρονεῖ.

Trachiniae, lines 441–442.

The champion who would square up to Love
Is ill-advised.

In my whole baggage there is very little Aeschylus. Only four fragments, of which I will declare three.

$$\tau a \dot{v} \tau \acute{a} \ \tau o \iota \ \pi \lambda a \nu \omega \mu \acute{e} \nu \eta$$
$$\pi \rho \grave{o} s \ \ddot{a} \lambda \lambda o \tau' \ \ddot{a} \lambda \lambda o \nu \ \pi \eta \mu o \nu \grave{\eta} \ \pi \rho o \sigma \iota \zeta \acute{a} \nu \epsilon \iota.$$

Prometheus Bound, lines 277–278.

Verily affliction wanders abroad impartially, and alights upon all in turn.

τέχνη δ' ἀνάγκης ἀσθενεστέρα μακρῷ.

Prometheus Bound, line 514.

Art is far weaker than necessity.

This should be the motto of every Shakespearean production on the stage and of nearly every book and picture.

ἀλλ' ἡσύχαζε σαυτὸν ἐκποδὼν ἔχων,
ἐγὼ γὰρ οὐκ εἰ δυστυχῶ, τοῦδ' εἵνεκα
θέλοιμ' ἂν ὡς πλείστοισι πημονὰς τυχεῖν.

Prometheus Bound, lines 346–348.

Go thou in peace: absent thee from this woe;
For though I suffer, not on that account
Would I have all the world made miserable.

Edward Marsh.

c

A fragment from Simonides:

ὡς ὁπόταν χειμέριον κατὰ μῆνα πινύσκῃ
Ζεὺς ἄματα τέσσαρα καὶ δέκα,
λαθάνεμόν τέ μιν ὥραν καλέοισιν ἐπιχθόνιοι
ἱρὰν παιδοτρόφον ποικίλας
ἀλκυόνος.

As when in the winter months Zeus brings fourteen days
of calm, and mortals call it the sacred, windless breeding
time of the many-coloured king-fisher.

An epigram by Rufinus:

πέμπω σοί, 'Ροδόκλεια, τόδε στέφος, ἄνθεσι καλοῖς
   αὐτὸς ὑφ' ἡμετέραις πλεξάμενος παλάμαις·
ἔστι κρίνον ῥοδέη τε κάλυξ νοτερή τ' ἀνεμώνη
   καὶ νάρκισσος ὑγρὸς καὶ κυαναυγὲς ἴον·
ταῦτα στεψαμένη λῆξον μεγάλαυχος ἐοῦσα·
   ἀνθεῖς καὶ λήγεις καὶ σὺ καὶ ὁ στέφανος.

It has been translated by many people. Here is mine:

Rhodocleia, flowers of spring
I have woven in a ring;
Take this wreath my offering.
Here's the lily, here the rose
Her full chalice shall disclose;
Frail narcissus; wet with dew,
Windflower, and the violet blue.
Wear the garland I have made;
Crowned with it, put pride away;
This wreath that blooms to-day must fade;
Thou thyself must fade some day.

Rufinus lived at Byzantium under the reign of the Emperor
Justinian, A.D. 530. He was called Rufinus Domesticus, which
meant he was a public servant—a domestic was the head of
each of the chief departments of the Imperial Service—and
was a high official. He must have seen the famous Empress
Theodora. I often fancy he must have been like one of the poets
who had official positions during the reign of Alexander III
in Russia.

That finishes Greek for the present. Other scraps may turn up later. Now as to Latin. Lucretius comes first, with a passage ending up with one of the most beautiful lines in literature:

Sed quasi naufragiis magnis multisque coortis
disiectare solet magnum mare transtra cavernas
antemnas proram malos tonsasque natantis,
per terrarum omnis oras fluitantia aplustra
ut videantur et indicium mortalibus edant,
infidi maris insidias virisque dolumque
ut vitare velint, neve ullo tempore credant
subdola cum ridet placidi pellacia ponti.

De Rerum Natura, Book II, lines 552–559.

As when great shipwrecks mark the tempest's might,
And planks and helms are tossing on the tide
With spars and prows and masts and drifting oars,
And many a hull goes floating by far shores,
A visible sign to mortals who would brave
The guileful ocean's treacherous strength and spite,
Bidding beware, nor evermore confide
In the false whisper of the windless wave.

H. S. Salt, *Treasures of Lucretius*, 1912.

Here is another more literal translation made by Edward Marsh and myself:

But as when many and great wrecks befall
The great sea tosses bench, ribs, yard, and prow,
And masts and floating oars; and gilded poops
Come drifting to the shores of all the world,
That men may see and by that warning shun
The wiles, the might, the treachery of waters,
Nor let themselves at any time be lured
With the sly magic of a smiling sea.

Then there is a passage about the gods:

> *Apparet divum numen sedesque quietae*
> *quas neque concutiunt venti nec nubila nimbis*
> *aspergunt, neque nix acri concreta pruina*
> *cana cadens violat, semperque innubilus aether*
> *integit et large diffuso lumine ridet.*
>
> Book III, lines 18–22.

This passage has been paraphrased by Tennyson:

> The Gods, who haunt
> The lucid interspace of world and world,
> Where never creeps a cloud, or moves a wind,
> Nor ever falls the least white star of snow,
> Nor ever lowest roll of thunder moans,
> Nor sound of human sorrow mounts to mar
> Their sacred everlasting calm!

There is no Horace in any of my notebooks, but there are many scraps of him in my memory. Even school did not spoil Horace for me. He opened the door on Italian landscape. He was not the first to do it. Macaulay, learnt by heart in childhood, preceded him with his *Lays of Ancient Rome*, and their unforgettable pictures of Italy:

> From many a lonely hamlet
>   Which, hid by beech and pine,
> Like an eagle's nest, hangs on the crest
>   Of purple Apennine,

or

> From where sweet Clanis wanders
>   Through corn and vines and flowers:
> From where Cortona lifts to heaven
>   Her diadem of towers,

and most evocative of all:

> The harvest of Arretium,
>   This year, old men shall reap;
> This year, young boys in Umbro
>   Shall plunge the struggling sheep;
> And in the vats of Luna,
>   This year, the must shall foam
> Round the white feet of laughing girls
>   Whose sires have marched to Rome.

Horace's *Odes* called up the same kind of pictures:

> *Unde si Parcae prohibent iniquae,*
> *dulce pellitis ovibus Galaesi*
> *flumen et regnata petam Laconi*
>   *rura Phalantho.*

Odes II. vi.

> Or let me seek Galesus' rills
>   (If this the envious Fates withhold),
> Sweet to the flocks that range the hills
>   Where brave Phalanthus reigned of old.

Lord Ravensworth.

It is idle to speculate which is the most perfect, or which are the most perfect, of Horace's odes. Some will be most attracted by his melancholy note, by that ode which begins with the most poignantly melancholy of all lines:

Eheu fugaces, Postume, Postume,
labuntur anni nec pietas moram
   rugis et instanti senectae
      adferet indomitaeque morti:

non si trecenis quotquot eunt dies,
amice, places illacrimabilem
   Plutona tauris, qui ter amplum
      Geryonen Tityonque tristi

compescit unda, scilicet omnibus,
quicumque terrae munere vescimur,
   enaviganda, sive reges
      sive inopes erimus coloni.

frustra cruento Marte carebimus
fractisque rauci fluctibus Hadriae,
   frustra per autumnos nocentem
      corporibus metuemus Austrum:

visendus ater flumine languido
Cocytos errans et Danai genus
   infame damnatusque longi
      Sisyphus Aeolides laboris:

linquenda tellus et domus et placens
uxor, neque harum quas colis arborum
   te praeter invisas cupressos
      ulla brevem dominum sequetur:

absumet heres Caecuba dignior
servata centum clavibus et mero
   tinget pavimentum superbo,
      pontificum potiore cenis.

Odes II. xiv.

[61]

I had heard all my life of a translation of this ode, which was said to begin:

> Eheu fugaces, Postume, Postume!
> Ah, for the years that are lost to me, lost to me!

I was told this was by Thackeray, but I could not find it, even in *Notes and Queries*, until it was run to earth for me in a book of quotations.

The lines are by R. H. Barham, the author of the *Ingoldsby Legends*, and they are called *Epigram*:

> What Horace says is—
> Eheu fugaces
> Anni labuntur, Postume, Postume!
> Years glide away and are lost to me, lost to me!
> Now, when the folks in the dance sport their merry toes,
> Taglionis and Ellslers; Duvernays and Ceritos,
> Sighing, I murmur, "O mihi praeteritos!"

I imagine he transposed *labuntur anni* to *anni labuntur* on purpose, on account of the rhythm in English. That is all there is of it.

Once during the War, while waiting when Generals were at a conference, in some village in the north of France, I translated the ode myself. Here is my version:

> Oh, Posthumus, my Posthumus, alas!
> The nimble-footed years, they pass, they pass....
>   Not all thy virtues will prevent
>   Old Age, nor bid cold Death relent.
>
> Though Hecatombs thou slaughter thrice a day,
> Yet Pluto, the untearful, claims his prey,
>   Who holds in his dominion
>   The triple-headed Geryon,
>
> And Tityus by the melancholy floss,
> Which all who taste the fruits of earth must cross;
>   Though mighty monarchs they should be
>   Or painful sons of husbandry.

[62]

In vain we shun the grievous wounds of war,
The angry Adriatic's surge and roar;
    And from the hot Sirocco hide,
    That threatens us at Autumntide.

We must behold thy tide creep on apace,
Cocytus, and the shameful Danaan race,
    And Sisyphus condemned to ply
    A hopeless task eternally;

And bid farewell for ever to the earth,
To wife and home, the land which gave us birth;
    Of all thy trees none follow thee
    Except the hated cypress-tree.

A worthier heir shall drain to the last lees
Those casks now guarded by a hundred keys,
    And drench the floor with wine more rare
    Than priests for festal days prepare.

Some people would be most moved by the stanzas on **Regulus:**

> *Fertur pudicae coniugis osculum*
> *parvosque natos ut capitis minor*
>   *ab se removisse et virilem*
>   *torvus humi posuisse vultum,*
>
> *donec labantis consilio patres*
> *firmaret auctor numquam alias dato,*
>   *interque maerentis amicos*
>   *egregius properaret exsul.*
>
> *atqui sciebat quae sibi barbarus*
> *tortor pararet; non aliter tamen*
>   *dimovit obstantis propinquos*
>   *et populum reditus morantem*
>
> *quam si clientum longa negotia*
> *diiudicata lite relinqueret,*
>   *tendens Venafranos in agros*
>   *aut Lacedaemonium Tarentum.*

Odes III. v.

c*

Andrew Lang writes about these stanzas thus: "That poem could only have been written by a Roman! The strength, the tenderness, the noble and monumental resolution and resignation —these are the gifts of the lords of human things, the masters of the world."

His translation of the stanzas in prose seems to me more satisfactory than any of the versions in verse which I have seen, as satisfactory as the translation made by Mr King to his class in Kipling's *Stalky and Co.*

> They say he put aside from him the pure lips of his wife and his little children, like a man unfree, and with his brave face bowed earthward sternly he waited till with such counsel as never mortal gave he might strengthen the heart of the Fathers, and through his mourning friends go forth, a hero, into exile.
>
> Yet well he knew what things were being prepared for him at the hands of the tormentors, who, none the less, put aside the kinsmen that barred his path and the people that would fain have delayed his return, passing through their midst as he might have done if, his retainers' weary business ended and the suits adjudged, he was faring to his Venafran lands or to Dorian Tarentum.

Others will be attracted by the melancholy dignity of

> *Non ego perfidum*
> *dixi sacramentum: ibimus, ibimus,*
> *utcumque praecedes, supremum*
> *carpere iter comites parati.*
>
> Odes II. xvii.

> No idle oath
> Has Horace sworn; whene'er you go,
> We both will travel, travel both
> The last dark journey down below.
>
> John Conington.

What one can safely say is this, that among his most perfect

[64]

odes there is none more perfect than that written to the Fountain Bandusia:

> *O fons Bandusiae splendidior vitro,*
> *dulci digne mero non sine floribus,*
>   *cras donaberis haedo,*
>   *cui frons turgida cornibus*
>
> *primis et Venerem et proelia destinat,*
> *frustra: nam gelidos inficiet tibi*
>   *rubro sanguine rivos*
>   *lascivi suboles gregis.*
>
> *te flagrantis atrox hora Caniculae*
> *nescit tangere, tu frigus amabile*
>   *fessis vomere tauris*
>   *praebes et pecori vago.*
>
> *fies nobilium tu quoque fontium,*
> *me dicente cavis impositam ilicem*
>   *saxis, unde loquaces*
>   *lymphae desiliunt tuae.*
>
> *Odes* III. xiii.

I translated it into blank verse:

> Spring of Bandusia,
> Red wine and festal garlands are thy meed.
> To-morrow I shall offer thee a kid
> For whom his waxing brow and budding horns
> Foretell both love and war.
> But all in vain; the blood of this wild offspring
> Thine icy waters must incarnadine.
>
> The dogstar, and the incandescent days
> Can parch thee not; and weary of the plough,
> The oxen and the silly sheep astray
> Shall find in thee delicious cool retreat.
>
> Thou shalt be numbered amongst famous springs:
> The rocks, the ilex, whence thy ripples fall
> Tinkling, shall live forever in my verse.

Horace is untranslatable; but although everyone is aware of this fact, the task is one which tempts everybody; Prime Ministers and statesmen such as Canning and Gladstone, novelists such as Bulwer Lytton, bankers such as T. C. Baring, great poets such as Milton and Dryden, and lesser poets such as Whyte Melville. And why not? It is a harmless occupation, and personally I greatly enjoy reading translations of Horace, however inadequate they are. We used to be told at school that the most untranslatable of all the odes was the famous ode to Pyrrha. Here is the untranslatable Latin:

Quis multa gracilis te puer in rosa
perfusus liquidis urget odoribus
    grato, Pyrrha, sub antro?
      cui flavam religas comam

simplex munditiis? heu quotiens fidem
mutatosque deos flebit et aspera
    nigris aequora ventis
      emirabitur insolens,

qui nunc te fruitur credulus aurea,
qui semper vacuam, semper amabilem
    sperat, nescius aurae
      fallacis! miseri, quibus

intemptata nites. me tabula sacer
votiva paries indicat uvida
    suspendisse potenti
      vestimenta maris deo.

Odes I. v.

I remember the schoolmaster I was up to telling us that Milton had translated this ode and had failed, failed miserably. I did not understand then, and I do not understand now, what the failure consisted in, except that Milton in this case does not use the vernacular, but appears to translate Latin not into English but into Latin-English. But as someone once said to me, when I made this objection: "He wrote *Paradise Lost* in a kind of Latin-English." Thomas Hood translated the ode, and so did

Sir Stephen de Vere. In this translation which I made myself,
I have attempted to avoid all Latin constructions.

> What youth as fresh as any flower,
> Pyrrha, is sighing in your bower:
> For whom is tied that yellow hair
> With careless care?
>
> How often shall he cry, alas!
> That faith and truth are frail as glass,
> And gasp when gales...no seaman he!...
> Convulse the sea.
>
> He dreams you golden to the end,
> Forever fancy-free, his friend,
> Nor knows what tricks the zephyrs play—
> Most hapless they
>
> For whom as yet untried you shine!
> My dripping clothes still salt with brine
> (The votive tablet proves the vow)
> Are Neptune's now.

No sooner had I made this translation than I was conscious
that I had left out several essential points and lights and shadows
of the original; so I made another:

> What blue-eyed boy is wooing you
> Amongst the roses and the dew
> Of some delicious grot,
> Pyrrha? For whom, Oh! dazzling snare!
> So carelessly you twist your hair
> In any simple knot?
>
> Alas! How often will he cry
> That fair is foul and gods can lie,
> And stare in wild dismay;
> When the black storm-clouds blot the skies,
> And blind his inexperienced eyes
> With bitter spray.

He thinks you golden to the core
And fancy-free for evermore,
(Poor boy!) forever true!
How lightly comes, how lightly goes
The breeze of love he little knows!
Poor boy, I pity you

Who nothing know yet of that sea
Save that it glitters. As for me,
Neptune can testify
My votive tablet decks his shrine;
My clothes still dripping with the brine:—
Once bitten is twice shy.

And no sooner had I finished this than I was conscious that it was too wordy: in fact, a paraphrase. Thus is the path of the translator beset with pitfalls, and such is his lot: to fail. *Simplex munditiis* is the phrase that has baffled all translators.

In the year 1909 in Paris, I remember Madame Bulteau (who wrote novels, and articles in the *Figaro* under the pseudonym of Femina) discussing who were the best contemporary writers of French prose. She said they were Anatole France (who, strange as it may seem to the present generation, was admired in those days) and Gérard d'Houville (Madame Henri de Régnier); but whereas, she said, in Anatole France's prose "on sent le soin, Gérard d'Houville écrit comme une femme qui se coiffe avec un tour de main". *Simplex munditiis*.

But as an instance of what seems to me a successful translation—successful in the sense that the reader would in reading the poem admire it in itself, whether he knew the original or not, and those who knew the original would not be unsatisfied—here is a famous ode, and a translation by Cowper:

> *Persicos odi, puer, apparatus,*
> *displicent nexae philyra coronae;*
> *mitte sectari, rosa quo locorum*
> *   sera moretur.*

[68]

simplici myrto nihil allabores
sedulus curo: neque te ministrum
dedecet myrtus neque me sub arta
vite bibentem.

Odes I. xxxviii.

Boy, I hate their empty shows,
    Persian garlands I detest,
Bring not me the late-blown rose
    Lingering after all the rest.

Plainer myrtle pleases me
    Thus outstretched beneath my vine,
Myrtle more becoming thee,
    Waiting with thy master's wine.

My favourite lines of Horace are the last stanza of the ode to the Ship, spoken, we used to be told at school, to the Ship of the State (I wonder?):

Nuper sollicitum quae mihi taedium,
nunc desiderium curaque non levis,
    interfusa nitentis
      vites aequora Cycladas.

Odes I. xiv.

The ode has been felicitously translated by Calverley, but I prefer Gladstone's translation of the last stanza:

Of old at best a weary weight,
A yearning care and constant strain of late,
    O shun the seas
That gird those glittering Cyclades.

Heredia, who possessed an Horatian perfection of phrase, wrote:

Et je ne verrai plus les riantes Cyclades.

Have I no Virgil to declare?

Virgil was spoilt for me once for all at school; I cannot think of him save through a mist of dreary "after-fours" on hot summer or cold winter afternoons, tedious combats between Turnus and some other Latin, and "saying lessons", which meant long and difficult passages to be learnt by heart. I have copied out of my own free will only a few lines of Virgil; besides these there are some that are engraved in my memory.

First of all, what are perhaps the most famous lines he wrote:

> *Quae regio in terris nostri non plena laboris?*
> *en Priamus. sunt hic etiam sua praemia laudi;*
> *sunt lacrimae rerum, et mentem mortalia tangunt.*
>
> *Aeneid*, Book I, lines 460–462.

These have been translated by Frederick Myers:

> What realm of earth, he answered, doth not know,
> O friend, our sad preeminence of woe?
> Tears waken tears, and honour honour brings,
> And mortal hearts are moved by mortal things.

Then earlier, in the same Book of the *Aeneid*:

> *O passi graviora, dabit deus his quoque finem.*
>
> *Aeneid*, Book I, line 199.

But I can find no translation of the line that gives one an inkling of the pathos of the original. The literal meaning is:

> You, who have suffered greater ills than these,
> Even to this shall God appoint an end.

Then come the famous lines about the ghosts on the shore of the river Acheron in the nether world, stretching out their arms in vain desire:

> *Stabant orantes primi transmittere cursum*
> *tendebantque manus ripae ulterioris amore,*
>
> *Aeneid*, Book VI, lines 313–314.

[70]

echoed by Belloc in one of his sonnets:

> Who bear their hands in suppliance with desire,
> With stretched desire for the ulterior shore,

and the equally famous lines to Marcellus:

> *Heu miserande puer, siqua fata aspera rumpas,*
> *tu Marcellus eris. manibus date lilia plenis,*
> *purpureos spargam flores animamque nepotis*
> *his saltem adcumulem donis et fungar inani*
> *munere,*
>
> *Aeneid*, Book VI, lines 882–886.

the last three translated by Myers thus:

> Give, give me lilies; thick the flowers be laid
> To greet that mighty, melancholy shade;
> With such poor gifts let me his praise maintain,
> And mourn with useless tears, and crown in vain.

Dryden gives the same passage thus:

> A new Marcellus shall arise in thee!
> Full canisters of fragrant lilies bring!
> Let me with funeral flowers his body strow;
> The gifts which parents to their children owe,
> This unavailing gift at least I may bestow!

I never "did" the *Georgics* at school, although I once had to copy out a whole *Georgic* for being late for something; so they are to me unspoilt, and I can read about the landscape in them, and enjoy it, as if such passages were written by a modern poet. For instance, *Georgics*, Book II, lines 485–489:

> *Rura mihi et rigui placeant in vallibus amnes,*
> *flumina amem silvasque inglorius. o ubi campi*
> *Spercheosque et virginibus bacchata Lacaenis*
> *Taygeta! o qui me gelidis convallibus Haemi*
> *sistat, et ingenti ramorum protegat umbra!*

[71]

translated by Myers:

> Still, Nature, let me still thy beauty know,
> Love the clear streams that thro' thy valleys flow,
> To many a forest lawn that love proclaim,
> Breathe the full soul, and make an end of fame!
> Ah me, Spercheos! Oh, to watch alway
> On Taygeta the Spartan girls at play!
> Or cool in Hæmus' gloom to feel me laid,
> Deep in his branching solitudes of shade!

This passage is most beautifully transposed by La Fontaine:

> Solitude, où je trouve une douceur secrète,
> Lieux que j'aimai toujours, ne pourrai-je jamais,
> Loin du monde et du bruit, goûter l'ombre et le frais?
> Oh! qui m'arrêtera sous vos sombres asiles?
> Quand pourront les neuf Sœurs, loin des cours et des villes,
> M'occuper tout entier, et m'apprendre des cieux
> Les divers mouvements inconnus à nos yeux,
> Les noms et les vertus de ces clartés errantes
> Par qui sont nos destins et nos mœurs différentes!
> Que si je ne suis né pour de si grands projets,
> Du moins que les ruisseaux m'offrent de doux objets!
> Que je peigne en mes vers quelque rive fleurie!
> La Parque à filets d'or n'ourdira point ma vie,
> Je ne dormirai point sous de riches lambris:
> Mais voit-on que le somme en perde de son prix?
> En est-il moins profond, et moins plein de délices?
> Je lui voue au désert de nouveaux sacrifices.
> Quand le moment viendra d'aller trouver les morts,
> J'aurai vécu sans soins, et mourrai sans remords.

Fables, Book XI, iv.

Then there is the exquisite picture of Italian cities:

> *Adde tot egregias urbes operumque laborem,*
> *tot congesta manu praeruptis oppida saxis*
> *fluminaque antiquos subterlabentia muros,*

Georgics, Book II, lines 155-157.

[72]

translated by Dryden:

> Next add our cities of illustrious name,
> Their costly labour, and stupendous fame;
> Our forts on steepy hills, that far below
> See wanton streams in winding valleys flow.

Another landscape in two lines:

> *Propter aquam tardis ingens ubi flexibus errat*
> *Mincius et tenera praetexit arundine ripas.*
>
> Georgics, Book III, lines 14–15.

By the water-side where mighty Mincius wanders, with links and loops, and fringes all the banks with the tender reed.

Andrew Lang.

This recalls Milton:

Smooth-sliding Mincius crowned with vocal reeds.

The beginning of the xth *Eclogue*:

> *Extremum hunc, Arethusa, mihi concede laborem.*
> *pauca meo Gallo, sed quae legat ipsa Lycoris,*
> *carmina sunt dicenda: neget quis carmina Gallo?*
> *sic tibi, cum fluctus subterlabere Sicanos,*
> *Doris amara suam non intermisceat undam:*
> *incipe; sollicitos Galli dicamus amores,*
> *dum tenera attondent simae virgulta capellae.*
> *non canimus surdis, respondent omnia silvae.*
> *quae nemora aut qui vos saltus habuere, puellae*
> *Naiades, indigno cum Gallus amore peribat?*
> *nam neque Parnasi vobis iuga, nam neque Pindi*
> *ulla moram fecere, neque Aonie Aganippe.*
> *illum etiam lauri, etiam flevere myricae,*
> *pinifer illum etiam sola sub rupe iacentem*
> *Maenalus et gelidi fleverunt saxa Lycaei.*
> *stant et oves circum (nostri nec paenitet illas,*
> *nec te paeniteat pecoris, divine poeta:*

et formosus ovis ad flumina pavit Adonis),
venit et upilio, tardi venere subulci,
uvidus hiberna venit de glande Menalcas.
omnes "unde amor iste" rogant "tibi?" venit Apollo:
"Galle, quid insanis?" inquit. "tua cura Lycoris
perque nives alium perque horrida castra secutast."
venit et agresti capitis Silvanus honore
florentis ferulas et grandia lilia quassans.
Pan deus Arcadiae venit, quem vidimus ipsi
sanguineis ebuli bacis minioque rubentem.

florentis ferulas et grandia lilia quassans has always seemed to
me one of the most magical of Virgil's lines. Shelley began a
beautiful translation of the passage:

Melodious Arethusa, o'er my verse
   Shed thou once more the spirit of thy stream:
Who denies verse to Gallus? So, when thou
   Glidest beneath the green and purple gleam
Of Syracusan waters, mayst thou flow
   Unmingled with the bitter Doric dew!
Begin, and, whilst the goats are browsing now
   The soft leaves, in our way let us pursue
The melancholy loves of Gallus. List!
   We sing not to the dead: the wild woods knew
His sufferings, and their echoes. . . .
   Young Naiads,. . .in what far woodlands wild
Wandered ye when unworthy love possessed
   Your Gallus? Not where Pindus is up-piled,
Nor where Parnassus' sacred mount, nor where
   Aonian Aganippe expands. . .
The laurels and the myrtle-copses dim.
   The pine-encircled mountain, Mænalus,
The cold crags of Lycæus, weep for him;
   And Sylvan, crowned with rustic coronals,
Came shaking in his speed the budding wands
   And heavy lilies which he bore: we knew
Pan the Arcadian.

I find in my luggage another scrap of Dryden's translation which I have always kept, without knowing to which poem it belonged till I looked it up lately.

> Plains, meads and orchards all the day he plies;
> The gleans of yellow thyme distend his thighs:
> He spoils the saffron flowers; he sips the blues
> Of violets, wilding blooms, and willow dews.

> *Crura thymo plenae; pascuntur et arbuta passim*
> *et glaucas salices casiamque crocumque rubentem*
> *et pinguem tiliam et ferrugineos hyacinthos.*
> > Georgics, Book IV, lines 181–183.

Then comes Catullus,

Tenderest of Roman poets nineteen hundred years ago,

who alone of the Latin poets gave and gives me as much pleasure to read—a pleasure the same in kind and in degree— as I get from reading an English, French or German poet. I have only once written out a poem of Catullus, but many of his lines are stored in my memory. There are the lines to Calvus on the death of Quintilia, so like (I fancy many people have noticed this) a sonnet of Shakespeare:

> *Si quicquam mutis gratum acceptumve sepulcris*
> *accidere a nostro, Calve, dolore potest,*
> *quo desiderio veteres renovamus amores*
> *atque olim missas flemus amicitias,*
> *certe non tanto mors immatura dolori'st*
> *Quintiliae, quantum gaudet amore tuo.*

It is the third and fourth lines which recall Shakespeare's:

> Then can I drown an eye, unus'd to flow,
> For precious friends hid in death's dateless night,
> And weep afresh Love's long since cancell'd woe,
> And moan the expense of many a vanish'd sight.

Equivalents such as these are the only translations of the Classics that are to my mind satisfactory. It is not possible to *translate* a pentameter such as

Pallidulum manans alluit unda pedem.

If you turn to an English scholar's translation of the passage where this line occurs—and the translation could not be bettered for accuracy—you find he renders it thus:

So lately the creeping wave of the Lethæan flood laps my own brother's death-pale foot, on whom, torn from my sight, the Trojan earth under the shore of Rhœteum lies heavy.

There is no fault to be found with the translation, except that we do not now, nor did we at any time, speak of a death-pale foot, and the whole construction reminds one of Latin, not English, and is obviously a translation from a dead tongue, which, after all, is what it sets out to be. It is not meant to be a "rendering".

Here is the text of the whole poem:

Etsi me assiduo confectum cura dolore
sevocat a doctis, Ortale, virginibus,
nec potis est dulcis Musarum expromere fetus
mens animi, tantis fluctuat ipsa malis:
namque mei nuper Lethaeo in gurgite fratris
pallidulum manans alluit unda pedem,
Troia Rhoeteo quem subter litore tellus
ereptum nostris obterit ex oculis.
alloquar, audiero numquam tua facta loquentem,
numquam ego te, vita frater amabilior,
aspiciam posthac. at certe semper amabo,
semper maesta tua carmina morte canam,
qualia sub densis ramorum concinit umbris
Daulias, absumpti fata gemens Ityli.
sed tamen in tantis maeroribus, Ortale, mitto
haec expressa tibi carmina Battiadae,
ne tua dicta vagis nequiquam credita ventis
effluxisse meo forte putes animo.

[77]

ut missum sponsi furtivo munere malum
  procurrit casto virginis e gremio,
quod miserae oblitae molli sub veste locatum,
  dum adventu matris prosilit, excutitur:
atque illud prono praeceps agitur decursu,
  huic manat tristi conscius ore rubor.

Four lines are said to be missing after the eighth line.

I have sometimes wondered whether one could not have a prose translation of this poem written in the vernacular, in English as she is spoke. The poem is an elegy on the death of Catullus' brother. I once attempted to translate it into ordinary English:

> Although I am harassed by undiminished grief, Hortalus, and sorrow has shut the door upon the Muse, nor can my heart find an outlet for its thoughts in verse, buffetted as it is by so great a trouble;—for but a little while ago the tide of Lethe crept up to the lifeless foot of my brother; and now we shall never see him again, and he lies under Trojan earth on the shore of Rhoeteum.
>
> Never more shall I speak to you again, never more shall I hear you tell of your doings, never shall I set eyes on you again, brother, dearer than life. But be sure I shall always love you, be sure I shall always sing songs of sorrow for your death, as under the dark shade of the boughs the nightingale bewails the fate of the lost Itylus.
>
> Yet in the midst of my great sorrow, Hortalus, I send you these lines of Battiades, which I translated for you, lest you should think your wish, "wind-dispersed and vain," had escaped my memory; as an apple sent in secret by her betrothed falls out from the chaste bosom of a girl (poor child, she had forgotten it!)—hidden in the soft folds of her gown, it is shaken out as she starts at the approach of her mother; the apple slips down and rolls away on the ground, and the maiden blushes for shame and casts down her eyes.

Catullus combines in the highest degree three great lyrical factors: passion, pathos, and grace.

Myers, in talking of Lucretius, said he "had painted, with all the mastering force of Rome, the pangs of passion baffled by its own intensity and festering unsated in a heart at war". This description seems to me to apply equally well to Catullus.

There is no more passionate poem in the world than the following:

Siqua recordanti benefacta priora voluptas
    est homini, cum se cogitat esse pium,
nec sanctam violasse fidem, nec foedere in ullo
    divum ad fallendos numine abusum homines,
multa parata manent in longa aetate, Catulle,
    ex hoc ingrato gaudia amore tibi.
nam quaecumque homines bene cuiquam aut dicere possunt
    aut facere, haec a te dictaque factaque sunt;
omnia quae ingratae perierunt credita menti.
    quare iam te cur amplius excrucies?
quin tu animo offirmas atque istinc te ipse reducis,
    et dis invitis desinis esse miser?
difficile est longum subito deponere amorem.
    difficile est, verum hoc qualubet efficias:
una salus haec est, hoc est tibi pervincendum,
    hoc facias, sive id non pote sive pote.
o di, si vestrum est misereri, aut si quibus umquam
    extremam iam ipsa in morte tulistis opem,
me miserum aspicite et, si vitam puriter egi,
    eripite hanc pestem perniciemque mihi,
si mihi surrepens imos ut torpor in artus
    expulit ex omni pectore laetitias.
non iam illud quaero, contra ut me diligat illa,
    aut, quod non potis est, esse pudica velit:
ipse valere opto et taetrum hunc deponere morbum.
    o di, reddite mi hoc pro pietate mea.

The following literal translation I made myself:

If it can please a man to recollect
His deeds of kindness done, and to reflect
That he has shown true loyalty in act
And word unto his friends, nor in a pact

Misused the gods to cheat his fellow men,
Your unrequited love should earn you then,
Catullus, life-long joys in overflow;
For what of kindness man to man may show,
In word or deed was said and done by you:
All this was given to a heart untrue:
And it is lost: then wherefore, spirit-sore,
Torment yourself with anguish any more?
Nay, stand entrenched within your peace to be,
And doff, despite the gods, your misery.
'Tis hard to bid long-rooted love begone,
But must in this way or in that be done.
There alone safety lies! This, carry through:
This, if you can or cannot, you must do.
Ye gods, if mercy lives within your span,
If you have ever helped a dying man,
Look down upon me in my agony;
My life was clean, so take this plague from me.
Ah me! within my inmost bones a blight
Has crept, and in my heart killed all delight.
I ask no more that she be kind to me—
Nor become chaste, for that could never be;
Gods, from this festering wound give me release,
If I have ever served you, grant me peace.

It is in the Latin as close in utterance as the tightest of
Shakespeare's sonnets, and gives one the impression of
a man almost inarticulate, so much has he to say. It expresses
a crucifixion of the spirit and of the heart as excruciating as
what is sometimes expressed in the lyrics of Heine. Excruciating
is the right word for many of Catullus' lyrics. He uses it
himself:

> *Odi et amo; quare id faciam, fortasse requiris.*
> *nescio, sed fieri sentio et excrucior.*

I hate and love: maybe you wonder how that can be.
I know not, but I feel it happening, and I am in torment.

But it is the poets who accidentally, and not the translators who deliberately, give us the best, the only equivalents of Catullus' passion and pathos. For instance, this sonnet by Louise Labé which is inspired by the *Vivamus Mea Lesbia* of Catullus:

> Baise m'encor, rebaise moy et baise:
> Donne m'en un de tes plus sauoureus,
> Donne m'en un de tes plus amoureus:
> Ie t'en rendray quatre plus chaus que braise.
>
> Las, te plains tu? ça que ce mal i'apaise,
> En t'en donnant dix autres doucereus.
> Air si meslans nos baisers tant heureus
> Iouissons nous l'un de l'autre a notre aise.
>
> Lors double vie a chacun en suiura.
> Chacun en soy et son ami viura.
> Permets m'Amour penser quelque folie:
>
> Tousiours suis mal, viuant discrettement
> Et ne me puis donner contentement,
> Si hors de moy ne fay quelque saillie.

It is the poets, too, who give us the best equivalent of his grace. The following lines, taken from *Les Contemplations* of Victor Hugo, give us an example of the grace which is peculiar to Catullus, and of what is also characteristic of him, an image from nature accurately and beautifully observed:

> L'enfant, voyant l'aïeule à filer occupée,
> Veut faire une quenouille à sa grande poupée.
> L'aïeule s'assoupit un peu; c'est le moment.
> L'enfant vient par derrière, et tire doucement
> Un brin de la quenouille où le fuseau tournoie,
> Puis s'enfuit triomphante, emportant avec joie
> La belle laine d'or que le safran jaunit,
> Autant qu'en pourrait prendre un oiseau pour son nid.

The pathos of Catullus is twofold: that of his love-poems, of which I have already quoted one example; here is another:

> *Caeli, Lesbia nostra, Lesbia illa,*
> *illa Lesbia, quam Catullus unam*
> *plus quam se atque suos amavit omnes.*

O, Caelius, my Lesbia, that Lesbia, Lesbia whom alone
Catullus loves more than himself and all his own.

This is

un long sanglot tout chargé d'adieu.

Equivalents of the bitterness and intensity of his passion are
to be found in Heine; in this poem, for instance:

Ich unglücksel'ger Atlas! eine Welt,
Die ganze Welt der Schmerzen, muß ich tragen,
Ich trage Unerträgliches, und brechen
Will mir das Herz im Leibe.

Du stolzes Herz! du hast es ja gewollt!
Du wolltest glücklich sein, unendlich glücklich
Oder unendlich elend, stolzes Herz,
Und jetzo bist du elend.

I miserable Atlas, a whole world,
A universe of suffering, must bear.
The burden is unbearable, my heart
Is breaking in my body.

Proud heart, you had to have it your own way.
You asked for happiness beyond all bounds,
Or boundless misery. And now, proud heart,
You have the misery.

Or, even without Schubert's wonderful music, this:

Still ist die Nacht, es ruhen die Gassen,
In diesem Hause wohnte mein Schatz;
Sie hat schon längst die Stadt verlassen,
Doch steht noch das Haus auf demselben Platz.

Da steht auch ein Mensch und starrt in die Höhe,
Und ringt die Hände, vor Schmerzensgewalt;
Mir graust es, wenn ich sein Antlitz sehe—
Der Mond zeigt mir meine eigne Gestalt.

[82]

Du Doppelgänger, du bleicher Geselle!
Was äffst du nach mein Liebesleid,
Das mich gequält auf dieser Stelle,
So manche Nacht, in alter Zeit?

The night is still, the streets are quiet, this is the house where she used to live; she left the town a long time ago, but the house still stands where it used to be.

And there stands a man staring upwards, and he wrings his hands in pain; I shudder when I see his face, it is myself that the moon shows to me.

Thou wraith, thou pale companion, how darest thou ape the sorrow of my love, which on this same spot racked me night after night in the days gone by?

Or this:

Sie hatten sich beide so herzlich lieb,
Spitzbübin war sie, er war ein Dieb.
Wenn er Schelmenstreiche machte,
Sie warf sich aufs Bett und lachte.

Der Tag verging in Freud' und Lust,
Des Nachts lag sie an seiner Brust.
Als man ins Gefängnis ihn brachte,
Sie stand am Fenster und lachte.

Er ließ ihr sagen: "O komm zu mir,
Ich sehne mich so sehr nach dir,
Ich rufe nach dir, ich schmachte—"
Sie schüttelt' das Haupt und lachte.

Um Sechse des Morgens ward er gehenkt,
Um Sieben ward er ins Grab gesenkt;
Sie aber schon um Achte
Trank roten Wein und lachte.

Lord Lytton translated the first two lines of this poem:

They loved each other beyond belief,
She was a harlot and he was a thief.

[83]

After the first two lines Lord Lytton, I think (I cannot find the poem), leaves the original altogether. I will translàte the rest of it in prose:

> Whenever he played his knavish tricks she threw herself on her bed and laughed. The day went by in joy and fun. At night she lay upon his breast. When they took him to prison, she stood at the window and laughed.
>
> He sent her a message: "Come to me. I long for you so dreadfully. I am crying for you, I can no more." She shook her head and laughed.
>
> At six in the morning they hanged him dead, at seven they laid him in his grave. But she, when the clock struck eight, drank red wine, and laughed.

There is another note, more solemn and more quiet, in the pathos of Catullus' verse: the note he sounds in his elegies, one of which, on his brother's death, I have already quoted. For this pathos, so simple and yet so poignant, I have found no equivalent; yet the dignity and the music of its expression are echoed by Swinburne in his *Ave Atque Vale* to Baudelaire:

> Thou art far too far for wings of words to follow,
>   Far too far off for thought or any prayer.
>   What ails us with thee, who art wind and air?
> What ails us gazing where all seen is hollow?
>   Yet with some fancy, yet with some desire,
>   Dreams pursue death, as winds a flying fire;
> Our dreams pursue our dead and do not find.

And then, after these lines, there occur, what we never find in Catullus, lines as musical, as perfect in sound, as those which have gone before, but otiose as to sense. Then follow two majestic stanzas, which are worthy of Catullus in quality and accent:

> Not thee, O never thee, in all time's changes,
>   Not thee, but this the sound of thy sad soul,
>   The shadow of thy swift spirit, this shut scroll
> I lay my hand on, and not death estranges
>   My spirit from communion of thy song—
>   These memories and these melodies that throng
> Veiled porches of a Muse funereal—
>   These I salute, these touch, these clasp and fold
>   As though a hand were in my hand to hold,
> Or through mine ears a mourning musical
>   Of many mourners rolled.
>
> I among these, I also, in such station
>   As when the pyre was charred, and piled the sods,
>   And offering to the dead made, and their gods,
> The old mourners had, standing to make libation,
>   I stand, and to the gods and to the dead
>   Do reverence without prayer or praise, and shed

Offering to these unknown, the gods of gloom,
  And what of honey and spice my seedlands bear,
  And what I may of fruits in this chilled air,
And lay, Orestes-like, across the tomb
  A curl of severed hair.

And then once again, as one continues, one is conscious of excess.
The whole poem, from its lovely opening:

Shall I strew on thee rose or rue or laurel,
  Brother, on this that was the veil of thee?
  Or quiet sea-flower moulded by the sea,
Or simplest growth of meadow-sweet or sorrel?

(then after the first fine lines the stanza becomes wordy
immediately) down to its noble close:

There lies not any troublous thing before,
Nor sight nor sound to war against thee more,
For whom all winds are quiet as the sun,
  All waters as the shore,

is a riot of musical syllables and a feast of lovely images, and
yet one is from time to time uneasily conscious that there is a
little too much of everything—too much sound, and not enough
sense—whereas in Catullus' elegies there is not a word too much,
and the emotion that beats in them is far more human and
far stronger.

I remember hearing Edmund Gosse in 1894 say that Swinburne
(and Swinburne had then been popular for twenty-nine years)
would in the future be a literary curiosity, like Cowley. When he
said this even some of the middle-aged disagreed; but it seems as
if his prophecy were coming true, at any rate in certain circles.
In the *New Book of English Verse*, the latest anthology, published
in 1935, a counterpart to the *Golden Treasury* (but handicapped
by not including anything inserted either in the *Golden Treasury*
or the *Oxford Book of English Verse*, and handicapped in its
own favour by allowing itself to quote passages from plays)
there is not one single poem by Swinburne.

But just as we are allowed to quote Cowley and admit that

he wrote one fine elegy, I suppose we are also allowed to quote Swinburne and admit that he wrote one great elegy.

Goethe said, "The English can say what they like about Byron, he is the greatest talent of the century."

People can say what they like about Swinburne, but one fact remains: he caught the ear, and excited to fever pitch the enthusiasm and delight, of more than one generation. He is locked in the temple of Fame, from which there is no escape, however often and however sharply its inmates suffer temporary eclipse. He shares with Byron and with Kipling the distinction of never having been thought a minor poet.

Byron and Kipling went farther, and conquered the reading public not only in England, but in Europe, and the world.

I should not be surprised if, when Swinburne is discovered by a future younger generation, they found some unminted gold in the little-known mines of his quite late work (in *Astrophel* for instance), some exquisite descriptions of English landscape, written in the Indian summer of his genius; when they do so, they will find an explorer has been there before them: Mrs Meynell.

D

I have no Tibullus to declare, and no Propertius. Ovid was spoilt for me at school, when we had not only to read the *Fasti*, but to try and emulate them. Ovid was despised, not only by my schoolmasters—although his verse was the only verse we were allowed to imitate—but also by such grown-up scholars as I came across. One of these said to me, when I was a Lower Boy at Eton, "I am sorry you have to read that *hog* Ovid." I believed him then; but now I no longer believe that Ovid was a hog. Once in the year 1909 I wrote two articles in *The Morning Post* in defence of French poetry; for in those curious days, incredible as it may seem, English professors and critics used to say that there was no such thing as French poetry, and that French poetry was not poetry. The article brought me a letter from George Wyndham, who said he had not known that anybody in England felt as he did in the matter. "I enjoy your argument", he wrote, "and hold your illustrations from Latin and Greek poetry to be conclusive. Even that battle has to be fought against young men from Balliol, just as if Catullus and Propertius had never lived, and as if Ovid were what boys were told he was, instead of an influence throughout the Middle Ages second—if at all—to Virgil, that classic and romantic rolled into one."

Schoolboys are more than bored by Ovid, they find him excruciatingly tedious; and grown-up scholars sometimes late in life get bored with Virgil (cf. Andrew Lang in *Letters on Literature*). In Anatole France's *Histoire Contemporaine* Monsieur Bergeret was engaged on a terribly tedious little book, that was never finished, called *Virgilius Nauticus*, and he confessed that he found nearly all Roman poets "terribles d'emphase et de médiocrité";* yet not for nothing did Ovid write, for he kindled sparks in the souls of Marlowe and Shakespeare. And as for Virgil, he not only lit that great blazing pyre we call Dante, but for many centuries he was worshipped like a god, and consulted like an oracle, and still across the dust of ages the leaves on his tree shine and gleam like gold and silver, and their rustling music moves the heart to tears. Frederick Myers, writing of a poignant passage in Virgil, says—and nobody has said it so well—

* Especially Virgil, *Aeneid*, Bk VIII.

These short and pregnant passages will appeal to different
minds with very different power. There are some whose
emotion demands a fuller expression than this, a more
copious and ready flow—who choose rather, like Shelley,
to pour the whole free nature into a sudden and untram-
melled lay. But there are others who have learnt to
recognise the last height of heroism, the last depth of
tenderness, rather in a word than in a protest, and rather
in a look than in a word; to whom all strong feeling
comes as a purging fire, a disengagement from the
labyrinth of things; whose passion takes a more concen-
trated dignity as it turns inwards and to the deep of the
heart. And such men will recognise in Virgil a precursor,
a master, and a friend; they will call him the *Magnanimo*,
the *Verace Duca*; they will enrol themselves with eager
loyalty among the spiritual progeny of a spirit so melancholy, august, and alone.

I believe that Ovid exercised as great an influence on Shake-
speare as Lemprière's Classical Dictionary and Chapman's Homer
did on Keats; but Shakespeare was probably not made to write
Latin verse nor taught to despise Ovid. I often wonder what a
Roman would think of the best efforts of European scholars
when writing Latin verse. Would it appear to them as the
English verse (sometimes full of beautiful ideas and images) of
a modern Indian appears to us; or as French verse written by
English-French scholars sounds to a Frenchman? My favourite
Latin poems written by Englishmen are Gray's fragment:

> *O lachrymarum fons, tenero sacros*
> *Ducentium ortus ex animo; quater*
> *Felix! in imo qui scatentem*
> *Pectore te, pia Nympha, sensit*

(the sentiment is Christian rather than Pagan, a fact which is under-
lined in the translation which Father Ronald Knox made for me:

> O Spring of tears, that, from a heart by grace
> Made tender, their divine procession trace!
> Happy, who from his bosom drawing deep
> That influence, dear Angel, learns to weep),

and Father Ronald Knox's pastiche of Calvus:

Pauper uterque, quibus non altera cura, parentes
  Quintiliae inferias rettulimus cineri,
non vocem audituri iterum, nec verba venusta,
  blaesiloquentis adhuc verba venusta tua.
qui tenerae placuere, sepulcro sternite flores:
  forsitan hoc etiam gaudeat ipsa cinis.

We her parents, poor in substance and having no other
love in life, have paid the last rites to Quintilia's ashes,
never again to hear that voice and those gay words—
those gay words of yours, still lisping. Cast on her tomb
the flowers her youth loved; maybe her very ashes will
take pleasure even in this.

These poems, and an elegy by Dean Inge, have always seemed
to my ignorant ear like real Latin poems, and not verses written
by clever sixth-form boys for competitions in the evening newspapers.

I have stepped straight from classical to modern Latin, having no Silver Latin to declare, but I could declare a piece of mediaeval Latin: the *Dies Irae*. I have read a great many translations of the *Dies Irae*. The one which to my mind renders most nearly the quality of the plangent sonorous treble-barrelled chords of the original is a translation by Swinburne, written at Oxford when he was very young. It is to be found in his posthumous poems:

> Day of wrath, the years are keeping,
> When the world shall rise from sleeping,
> With a clamour of great weeping!

> Earth shall fear and tremble greatly
> To behold the advent stately
> Of the Judge that judgeth straitly,

> And the trumpet's fierce impatience
> Scatter strange reverberations
> Thro' the graves of buried nations.

> Death and Nature will stand stricken
> When the hollow bones shall quicken
> And the air with weeping thicken,

> When the Creature, sorrow-smitten,
> Rises where the Judge is sitting
> And beholds the doom-book written.

> For, that so his wrath be slakèd,
> All things sleeping shall be wakèd,
> All things hidden shall be naked.

> When the just are troubled for thee,
> Who shall plead for me before thee,
> Who shall stand up to implore thee?

> Lest my great sin overthrow me,
> Let thy mercy, quickened thro' me,
> As a fountain overflow me!

> For my sake thy soul was movèd;
> For my sake thy name reprovèd,
> Lose me not whom thou hast lovèd!

Yea, when shame and pain were sorest,
For my love the cross thou borest,
For my love the thorn-plait worest.

By that pain that overbore thee,
By those tears thou weptest for me,
Leave me strength to stand before thee.

For the heart within me yearneth,
And for sin my whole face burneth;
Spare me when thy day returneth.

By the Magdalen forgiven,
By the thief made pure for heaven,
Even to me thy hope was given.

Tho' great shame be heavy on me,
Grant thou, Lord, whose mercy won me,
That hell take not hold upon me.

Thou whom I have lovèd solely,
Thou whom I have lovèd wholly,
Leave me place among the holy!

When thy sharp wrath burns like fire,
With the chosen of thy desire,
Call me to the crownèd choir!

Prayer, like flame with ashes blending,
From my crushed heart burns ascending;
Have thou care for my last ending.

He has not attempted to translate the great line:

Rex tremendae maiestatis,

but he gives the effect of the whole stanza in his stanza that
begins:

Lest my great sin overthrow me.

And what about Latin prose? The answer is, Hardly any.
There is a little Tacitus; the description of Nero's wife Poppæa
from the *Annals*.

Erat in civitate Sabina Poppæa, T. Ollio patre genita, sed no-

[92]

*men avi materni sumpserat, inlustri memoria Poppæi Sabini,
consulari et triumphali decore præfulgentis; nam Ollium
honoribus nondum functum amicitia Seiani pervertit. huic
mulieri cuncta alia fuere præter honestum animum. quippe
mater eius, ætatis suæ feminas pulchritudine supergressa,
gloriam pariter et formam dederat; opes claritudini generis
sufficiebant. sermo comis nec absurdum ingenium: mo-
destiam præferre et lascivia uti. rarus in publicum
egressus, idque velata parte oris, ne satiaret aspectum, vel
quia sic decebat. famæ nunquam pepercit, maritos et
adulteros non distinguens; neque adfectui suo aut alieno
obnoxia, unde utilitas ostenderetur, illuc libidinem trans-
ferebat.*

Annals, Book XIII, chapter 45.

There lived at that time at Rome Sabina Poppæa, the
daughter of Titus Ollius, but she assumed the name of
her maternal grandfather, Poppæus Sabinus of illustrious
memory.... This woman had every gift except that of
virtue. She had inherited from her mother, who was the
most beautiful woman of her age, beauty as well as fame;
and her fortune was adequate to her rank. She talked
well and sometimes wittily. She professed virtue and
practised vice. She went out but little, and then always
veiled, either to excite and then disappoint curiosity, or
because she knew it suited her. She cared nothing for
her reputation, and made no distinction between husbands
and paramours, and she never allowed her own affections
or those of others to interfere with her interests; where
these lay, thither did she transfer her favours.

This reads like a page of Maupassant or Bourget; the terseness
is incomparable.

Here is an example of his biting irony:

*Tardum Galbæ iter et cruentum, interfectis Cingonio
Varrone consule designato, et Petronio Turpiliano consulari: ille ut Nymphidii socius, hic ut dux Neronis,
inauditi atque indefensi, tamquam innocentes perierant.*

Histories, Book I, chapter 6.

Varro and Turpilianus were condemned unheard and undefended, so that they might just as well have been innocent.

And here is perhaps the original of Milton's line:

That last infirmity of noble mind,

Erant quibus appetentior famæ videretur, quando etiam sapientibus cupido gloriæ novissima exuitur.

Histories, Book IV, chapter 6.

Legioni classicæ diffidebatur.

Histories, Book I, chapter 31

The marines were distrusted.

Is this the origin of "Tell it to the marines"?

I have no more Latin to declare, and the Customs House officer passes on to Italian.

I have such a heavy trunk full of Dante that he says a few samples will do. I begin, not with the dawn, but with the hour before the dawn, in the *Purgatorio*, in that soft atmosphere which is all the more serene and beautiful for being reached through and after the fumes and fires of the *Inferno*.

"But", says the Customs House officer, "have you nothing to declare from the *Inferno*?" I say I could declare a great deal of it: first of all Paolo and Francesca: the most beautiful and most moving love-story ever written. "That", said the officer, "must be declared at once. It cannot be declared too often, for it is one of those passages which, however well it is known to the reader, is found, whenever it is read, once again to contain something new and unexpected."

> *Siede la terra, dove nata fui,*
> *Su la marina, dove 'l Po discende*
> *Per aver pace co' seguaci sui.*
> *Amor, ch' a cor gentil ratto s' apprende,*
> *Prese costui della bella persona*
> *Che mi fu tolta, e il modo ancor m' offende.*
> *Amor, ch' a null' amato amar perdona,*
> *Mi prese del costui piacer sì forte,*
> *Che, come vedi, ancor non m' abbandona.*
> *Amor condusse noi ad una morte:*
> *Caina attende chi vita ci spense!*
> *Queste parole da lor ci fur porte.*
> *Da ch' io intesi quell' anime offense,*
> *Chinai 'l viso, e tanto 'l tenni basso,*
> *Fin che 'l Poeta mi disse: Che pense?*
> *Quando risposi, cominciai: Oh lasso,*
> *Quanti dolci pensier, quanto disio*
> *Menò costoro al doloroso passo!*
> *Poi mi rivolsi a loro, e parla' io,*
> *E cominciai: Francesca, i tuoi martiri*
> *A lagrimar mi fanno tristo e pio.*
> *Ma dimmi: al tempo de' dolci sospiri,*

D*

A che, e come concedette Amore
Che conosceste i dubbiosi disiri?
Ed ella a me: "Nessun maggior dolore,
Che ricordarsi del tempo felice
Nella miseria; e ciò sa 'l tuo dottore.
Ma s' a conoscer la prima radice
Del nostro amor tu hai cotanto affetto,
Farò come colui che piange e dice.
Noi leggevamo un giorno per diletto
Di Lancillotto, come amor lo strinse:
Soli eravamo e senza alcun sospetto.
Per più fiate gli occhi ci sospinse
Quella lettura, e scolorocci 'l viso:
Ma solo un punto fu quel che ci vinse.
Quando leggemmo il disiato riso
Esser baciato da cotanto amante,
Questi, che mai da me non fia diviso,
La bocca mi baciò tutto tremante:
Galeotto fu il libro e chi lo scrisse:
Quel giorno più non vi leggemmo avante."
Mentre che l' uno spirto questo disse,
L' altro piangeva, sì, che di pietade
Io venni men, così com' io morisse;
E caddi, come corpo morto cade.

The passage has been translated by Byron:

"The land where I was born sits by the seas,
  Upon that shore to which the Po descends,
  With all his followers, in search of peace.
Love, which the gentle heart soon apprehends,
  Seized him for the fair person which was ta'en
  From me, and me even yet the mode offends.
Love, who to none beloved to love again
  Remits, seized me with wish to please, so strong,
  That, as thou seest, yet, yet it doth remain.
Love to one death conducted us along,
  But Caina waits for him our life who ended":
  These were the accents uttered by her tongue,—

Since I first listen'd to these souls offended,
    I bow'd my visage, and so kept it till—
    "What think'st thou?" said the bard; when I unbended,
And recommenced: "Alas! unto such ill
    How many sweet thoughts, what strong ecstasies,
    Led these their evil fortune to fulfil!"
And then I turn'd unto their side my eyes,
    And said, "Francesca, thy sad destinies
    Have made me sorrow till the tears arise.
But tell me, in the season of sweet sighs,
    By what and how thy love to passion rose,
    So as his dim desires to recognise?"
Then she to me: "The greatest of all woes
    Is to remind us of our happy days
    In misery, and that thy teacher knows.
But if to learn our passion's first root preys
    Upon thy spirit with such sympathy,
    I will do even as he who weeps and says.
We read one day for pastime, seated nigh,
    Of Lancilot, how love enchain'd him too.
    We were alone, quite unsuspiciously.
But oft our eyes met, and our cheeks in hue
    All o'er discolour'd by that reading were;
    But one point only wholly us o'erthrew;
When we read the long-sigh'd-for smile of her,
    To be thus kiss'd by such devoted lover,
    He who from me can be divided ne'er
Kiss'd my mouth, trembling in the act all over;
    Accursed was the book and he who wrote!
    That day no further leaf we did uncover."
While thus one spirit told us of their lot,
    The other wept, so that with pity's thralls
    I swoon'd, as if by death I had been smote,
And fell down even as a dead body falls.

The Customs House officer asks me if there is anything else.
I answer:

Farinata degli Uberti, Ulysses, Ugolino: I needn't show all

those, he replies, but I must show something more. So I choose
the lines about Brunetto Latini:

> *Poi si rivolse, e parve di coloro,*
> *Che corrono a Verona 'l drappo verde*
> *Per la campagna; e parve di costoro*
> *Quegli che vince, e non colui che perde.*

Then he turned and he seemed like those who race on
the plains at Verona for the green mantle; and of those
he seemed the man who wins the prize and not the man
who loses the race.

But to go back to the lines about the Dawn in the *Purgatorio*,
there is first of all the moment before the dawn, which Dante
describes, and in which he beholds for the first time, naturally
enough, as he is emerging at the Antipodes, the Southern Cross.
Some critics have said that he did not really mean the Southern
Cross, because in those days nobody knew there was such a
thing. Whether he meant it or not, he describes it in the following
words:

> *Dolce color d' oriental zaffiro,*
> > *Che s' accoglieva nel sereno aspetto*
> > *Dell' aer puro, infino al primo giro,*
> *Agli occhi miei ricominciò diletto,*
> > *Tosto ch' io usci' fuori dell' aura morta,*
> > *Che m' avea contristato gli occhi e 'l petto.*
> *Lo bel pianeta, ch' ad amar conforta,*
> > *Faceva tutto rider l' oriente,*
> > *Velando i Pesci, ch' erano in sua scorta.*
> *Io mi volsi a man destra, e posi mente*
> > *All' altro polo: e vidi quattro stelle*
> > *Non viste mai, fuor ch' alla prima gente.*

The oriental sapphire's lovely hue
That colour'd the pure air, serenely bright,
O'erspreading all the sky with deepest blue,
   Again unto mine eyes brought back delight;
Soon as the deathly air I rose above,
The air that grieved my heart and dimm'd my sight,

The beauteous planet, counsellor of love,
Arose and shed o'er all the east her smile,
Hiding the Fish that in her escort move.
  To the right hand I turn'd, and gazed awhile
At the far pole, and saw four stars, unseen
By man since sin our parents did beguile.

Mrs Ramsay.

A little later come lines on the dawn itself:

L'alba vinceva l'ora mattutina
Che fuggía innanzi sì che di lontano
Conobbi il tremolar della marina.

They are translated by Cary as follows:

The dawn had chased the matin hour of prime
Which fled before it, so that from afar
I spied the trembling of the ocean stream.

Mrs Ramsay translates it, more happily, I think, thus:

The dawn was conquering the mists that flee
Before it, as the early shadows wane;
Afar I knew the trembling of the sea.

There is in Catullus a beautiful equivalent to this:

Hic, qualis flatu placidum mare matutino
horrificans Zephyrus proclivis incitat undas,
aurora exoriente vagi sub limina Solis:
quae tarde primum clementi flamine pulsae
procedunt, leni et resonant plangore cachinni,
post vento crescente magis magis increbrescunt,
purpureaque procul nantes ab luce refulgent.

Hereupon, as the west wind ruffling the quiet sea with its
breath at morn urges on the sloping waves, when the
Dawn is rising up to the gates of the travelling Sun, the
waters, slowly at first, driven by gentle breeze, step on
and lightly sound with plash of laughter; then, as the
breeze grows fresh, they crowd on close and closer, and
floating afar, reflect a brightness from the crimson light.

F. W. Cornish.

Of all the landscape painters in verse, there is none who has a more magical touch than Dante, nor any who can evoke a more spacious picture with so few strokes. For instance,

> *E come li stornei ne portan l' ali,*
>   *Nel freddo tempo, a schiera larga e piena,*

> And as the starlings, borne upon the wing,
>   Fly in large flocks in the cold winter air,

or

> *Li ruscelletti che de' verdi colli*
>   *Del Casentin discendon giuso in Arno,*
>   *Faccendo i lor canali freddi e molli,*

> The rills, that glitter down the grassy slopes
> Of Casentino, making fresh and soft
> The banks whereby they glide to Arno's stream.

Cary.

And there is no writer who can concentrate so much deep feeling in such terse language. When Gray wrote "Thoughts that breathe and words that burn", I wonder if he had Dante in his mind. He was a Dante scholar, and lifted one of Dante's most beautiful lines into his *Elegy*; and there is no surer mark of a great poet than to be able to lift successfully. Just as the French say about witty sayings, "On ne les prête qu'aux riches", so is it only the very rich poets who steal from their fellow poets. The poor do not dare. The contrast would be too sharp between what they have written themselves and what they borrowed.

In the whole of the *Divine Comedy* there is to my mind no passage more tremendous in intensity and incandescent feeling than the apostrophe to Italy in the vith Canto of the *Purgatorio*, in which there is an inner apostrophe to Albert the Emperor:

> *O Alberto tedesco, ch' abbandoni*
>   *costei ch' è fatta indomita e selvaggia,*
>   *e dovresti inforcar li suoi arcioni,*
>   *giusto giudicio da le stelle caggia*
>   *sovra 'l tuo sangue, e sia novo ed aperto,*
>   *tal che 'l tuo successor temenza n' aggia!*

Ch' avete tu e 'l tuo padre sofferto,
per cupidigia di costà distretti,
che 'l giardin de lo 'mperio sia diserto.
Vieni a veder Montecchi e Cappelletti,
Monaldi e Filippeschi, om sanza cura:
color già tristi, e questi con sospetti!
Vien, crudel, vieni, e vedi la pressura
de' tuoi gentili, e cura lor magagne;
e vedrai Santafior com' è secura!
Vieni a veder la tua Roma che piagne
vedova e sola, e dì e notte chiama:
"Cesare mio, perchè non m' accompagne?"

This passage seems to me to combine the majesty of Virgil, the grandeur of Milton, the fire of Byron, and the felicity of Shakespeare. The verse translations of this passage, at least such as I have come across, seem to me pale. I will quote Mrs Ramsay's:

O German Albert, who forsakest her
Who all untamed and lawless has become,
While thou to ride this steed thy limbs shouldst stir,
    On thee and on thy race may righteous doom
Fall from on high, made clearly manifest,
That he may fear who cometh in thy room.
    Thou and thy father were in such hot haste
For distant conquest, that ye now permit
The garden of the empire to be waste.
    Come look on Montague and Capulet,
Monaldi, Filippeschi, heartless power!
And some do groan, some only fear as yet.
    Come, cruel, come, and thou shalt see how sore
The pains and sorrows by thy vassals borne;
And look how safe it is in Santafior!
    Come and behold thy Rome, who now doth mourn,
Lonely and widow'd; day and night she cries,
"My Caesar, wherefore leav'st thou me forlorn?"

Other lines which are marvellous in their beauty and Homeric completeness are:

> *A noi venia la creatura bella,*
> *Bianco vestita, e nella faccia quale*
> *Par tremolando mattutina stella.*

Then came that lovely being from afar,
Clothed in white robes, and bearing on his brow
The trembling glory of the morning star.

Mrs Ramsay.

Then, in the mysterious vision which visits Dante in the xixth Canto of the *Purgatorio*, there are those subtly melodious lines:

> *Io son, cantava, io son dolce sirena,*
> *Che i marinari in mezzo il mar dismago:*
> *Tanto son di piacere a sentir piena.*
>   *Io volsi Ulisse del suo cammin vago*
> *Al canto mio:*

She sang: "I am the siren of sweet sound,
Charming the mariners amid the sea,
For in my voice such melody is found.
I drew Ulysses from his path to me,
With my sweet singing."

Mrs Ramsay.

For pictorial effect there is nothing more lovely in the *Divine Comedy* than the description of the Earthly Paradise at the end of the *Purgatorio*, and the vision of Matilda picking flowers, like the Primavera of Botticelli:

> *Una Donna soletta che si gía*
> *Cantando ed iscegliendo fior da fiore,*
> *Ond' era pinta tutta la sua via.*

These lines have been translated by Shelley:

> A solitary woman! And she went
> Singing and gathering flower after flower,
> With which her way was painted and besprent.

Dante addresses her thus:

> *Tu mi fai rimembrar dove e qual era*
> *Proserpina, nel tempo che perdette*
> *La madre lei, ed ella primavera.*

> Thou seemest to my fancy, singing here
> And gathering flowers, as that fair maiden when
> She lost the spring, and Ceres her more dear.
>
> Shelley.

This vision is presently eclipsed by one still more beautiful, the apparition of Beatrice:

> *Così dentro una nuvola di fiori,*
> *Che dalle mani angeliche saliva,*
> *E ricadeva giù dentro e di fuori,*
> *Sovra candido vel cinta d' oliva*
> *Donna m' apparve, sotto verde manto*
> *Vestita di color di fiamma viva.*
> *E lo spirito mio, che già cotanto*
> *Tempo era stato, ch' alla sua presenza*
> *Non era di stupor tremando affranto,*
> *Sanza dagli occhi aver più conoscenza,*
> *Per occulta virtù, che da lei mosse,*
> *D' antico amor sentì la gran potenza.*

Mrs Ramsay translates the first six lines admirably:

> Even thus, within a cloud of blossoms bright,
> That, rising from those hands angelic, came,
> And fell around the chariot, in my sight,
>   With snow-white veil and olive diadem,
> A Lady I beheld, 'neath mantle green,
> Cloth'd in the colour of the living flame.

But after that the shackles of rhyme force her to use clichés; so Cary's translation of the end of the passage is more satisfactory:

> And o'er my spirit, that so long a time
> Had from her presence felt no shuddering dread,
> Albeit mine eyes discern'd her not, there moved
> A hidden virtue from her, at whose touch
> The power of ancient love was strong within me.

Then there comes a line and a half to me as exquisite as the supremest achievements in Chinese art, whether on porcelain or on silk; and I say Chinese advisedly, because they recall to me effects of Chinese landscape actually seen in Manchuria in the autumn twilight:

> Men che di rose e più che di viole
>   Colore aprendo.

The line is a description of blossom, and Dante says that, in the soft days of spring before the sun has become strong, blossom shines a little less than pink and more than mauve.

Now comes the *Paradiso,* of which there will be very little, for the simple reason that there is too much. Even in my notebooks there are long passages copied out. I will confine myself first of all to two lines which Matthew Arnold used to quote as a supreme example of the grand style, and which I consider unequalled in the poetry of the world. They are:

> *In la sua volontade è nostra pace:*
> *Ella è quel mare, al qual tutto si muove.*

Cary translates these lines:

> And in his will is our tranquillity:
> It is the mighty ocean, whither tends
> Whatever it creates and nature makes.

But the translation has not the great accent of the original.

In the XIIth Canto there occur two of the most musical lines Dante ever wrote:

> In quella parte, ove surge ad aprire
> Zeffiro dolce le novelle fronde.

When it is a question of the music of lines such as these, there is absolutely no point in appending a translation, for the sense is of no importance and the sound cannot be reproduced. Sometimes a translator by a miracle can raise either one or the other, or both; but in the case of these particular lines I have not been able to find anything remotely adequate.

In the XVIth Canto there are two lines:

> E come 'l volger del ciel della Luna
> Cuopre e discuopre i liti senza posa.

They remind me of Keats' great image:

> The moving waters at their priestlike task
> Of pure ablution round earth's human shores.

In the XVIIth Canto there is one of those passages where Dante, on the subject of exile, writes words of fire:

Tu lascerai ogni cosa diletta
Più caramente: e questo è quello strale
Che l' arco dell' esilio pria saetta.
  Tu proverai sì come sa di sale
Lo pane altrui, e com' è duro calle
Lo scendere e 'l salir per l' altrui scale.

This is Cary's translation:

Thou shalt leave each thing
Beloved most dearly: this is the first shaft
Shot from the bow of exile. Thou shalt prove
How salt the savour is of other's bread:
How hard the passage, to descend and climb
By other's stairs.

Scaling the circles of the *Paradiso*, we are conscious the whole time of an ascent not only in the quality of the substance but in that of the form. It is a long perpetual crescendo, increasing in beauty until the final consummation in the very last line. Somebody once defined an artist—I read this definition in a novel which was published anonymously—as a man who knew how to finish things. If this definition is true—and I think it is—then Dante was the greatest artist who ever lived. His final canto is the best, and it depends on and completes the beginning. Towards the end, but before the final vision of Beatitude, there is St Bernard's Hymn to Our Lady:

Vergine Madre, figlia del tuo Figlio,
Umile ed alta più che creatura,
Termine fisso d' eterno consiglio;
  Tu se' colei, che l' umana natura
Nobilitasti sì, che 'l suo Fattore
Non disdegnò di farsi sua fattura.
  Nel ventre tuo si raccese l' amore,
Per lo cui caldo, nell' eterna pace,
Così è germinato questo fiore.
  Qui se' a noi meridïana face
Di caritade; e giuso, intra i mortali,
Se' di speranza fontana vivace.

[106]

Donna, se' tanto grande e tanto vali,
Che qual vuol grazia, ed a te non ricorre,
Sua distanza vuol volar senz' ali.

La tua benignità non pur soccorre
A chi dimanda, ma molte fïate
Liberamente al dimandar precorre.

In te misericordia, in te pietate,
In te magnificenza, in te s' aduna
Quantunque in creatura è di bontate.

Or questi, che dall' infima lacuna
Dell' universo insin qui ha vedute
Le vite spiritali ad una ad una,

Supplica a te, per grazia, di virtute
Tanto, che possa con gli occhi levarsi
Più alto, verso l' ultima salute.

Ed io, che mai per mio veder non arsi
Più ch' io fo per lo suo, tutti i miei prieghi
Ti porgo (e prego che non sieno scarsi),

Perchè tu ogni nube gli disleghi
Di sua mortalità, co' prieghi tuoi,
Si che 'l sommo piacer gli si dispieghi.

Ancor ti prego, Regina che puoi
Ciò che tu vuoli, che conservi sani,
Dopo tanto veder, gli affetti suoi.

Vinca tua guardia i movimenti umani:
Vedi Beatrice, con quanti beati,
Per li miei prieghi ti chiudon le mani.

These lines have been twice beautifully imitated by Chaucer:
once at the beginning of the Tale of Cecilia, assigned in the
Canterbury Tales to the Second Nun, and once in the Prologue
to the *Prioress' Tale*, which I will quote:

O moder mayde! O mayde moder fre!
O bush unbrent, brenninge in Moyses sighte!
That ravisedest doun fro the Deitee,
Thurgh thyn humblesse, the Goost that in thalighte;

Of whos vertu, whan He thyn herte lighte,
Conceived was the Fadres sapience,
Help me to telle it in thy reverence!

Lady, thy bountee, thy magnificence,
Thy vertu, and thy grete humilitee,
Ther may no tonge expresse in no science;
For somtyme, lady, er men praye to thee,
Thou goost biforn of thy benignytee,
And getest us the light, thurgh thy preyere,
To gyden us unto thy Sone so deere.

My conning is so wayk, O blisful queene,
For to declare thy grete worthynesse,
That I ne may the weighte nat sustene;
But as a child of twelf monthe old or lesse,
That can unnethes any word expresse,
Right so fare I, and therfor I yow preye,
Gydeth my song that I shal of yow seye.

Did Shakespeare ever read Dante? There is a passage in
Measure for Measure which makes me think he may possibly
have read the *Inferno*:

> Ay, but to die, and go we know not where;
> To lie in cold obstruction, and to rot;
> This sensible warm motion to become
> A kneaded clod; and the delighted spirit
> To bathe in fiery floods, or to reside
> In thrilling regions of thick-ribbed ice;
> To be imprison'd in the viewless winds,
> And blown with restless violence round about
> The pendent world; or to be worse than worst
> Of those that lawless and incertain thoughts
> Imagine howling!—'tis too horrible,
> The weariest and most loathed worldly life,
> That age, ache, penury, and imprisonment
> Can lay on nature, is a paradise
> To what we fear of death.
>
> *Measure for Measure*, Act III, Scene 1.

You could find no better description or summary of the
punishments which Dante tells us of in the *Inferno* than some
of these lines; it is not unreasonable to believe that when
Shakespeare wrote

> To be imprison'd in the viewless winds,
> And blown with restless violence round about
> The pendent world

he may have had in his mind Dante's

> La bufera infernal, che mai non resta,

and Paolo and Francesca

> Together on the never-resting air.

Immediately after Dante in my luggage there occur fragments of Donne. When I first made the acquaintance of the literary, Edmund Gosse used to say that Donne would have been considered the greatest of all the English poets if we only had certain isolated lines to judge by; if we had, for instance, about as much of Donne as we have of Sappho. I have always thought this perfectly true, but unfortunately we have more. For instance, a poem such as *Air and Angels* has a beginning as wonderful as its title. Nothing could be better than the first six lines:

> Twice or thrice had I loved thee,
>   Before I knew thy face or name;
>   So in a voice, so in a shapeless flame,
>   Angels affect us oft, and worshipped be.
>   Still when, to where thou were, I came,
>   Some lovely glorious nothing did I see.

But after this the poem wanders off into a complicated maze of metaphysical conceits. The same thing is true of the *Relic* —if there were only the first stanza we should have thought, and rightly, that here was one of the greatest poets of the world. Here it is, copied out in 1898:

> When my grave is broke up again
> Some second guest to entertain,
>   —For graves have learn'd that woman-head
>   To be to more than one a bed—
>   And he that digs it spies
> A bracelet of bright hair about the bone,
>   Will not he let us alone,
> And think that there a loving couple lies,
> Who thought that this device might be some way
> To make their souls at the last busy day
> Meet at this grave and make a little stay?

And there are other beginnings which raise such wonderful hopes; for instance:

> By that first strange and fatal interview,

or:

> So, so break off this last lamenting kiss.

The only completely satisfying poem of Donne seems to me his *Hymn to God the Father*.

Sometimes he takes one's breath away by a sudden isolated image; for instance, the famous

> Doth not a Teneriffe or higher hill
> Rise so high like a rock, that one might think
> The floating moon would shipwreck there and sink?

or the famous ejaculation:

> I long to talk with some old lover's ghost
> Who died before the god of Love was born,

or:

> No spring nor summer beauty hath such grace
> As I have seen in one autumnal face.

or:

> 'Twere profanation of our joys
>   To tell the laity our love.

Mixed up with Donne in my luggage are two prose fragments written by Mrs Brewster, who was a German, in French. She was the wife of Henry Brewster, the author of *The Prison*, a book of philosophical dialogue. Édouard Rod published in Paris, after her death, a small collection of her notes called *Via Lucis*. They are of extreme beauty and delicacy. These two are both about death:

> *Tu te réveilléras, tu chercheras et ne trouveras plus personne. Tu te rappelleras que tu avais une mémoire, mais tu n'auras pas peur. Les mots seront effacés mais le rythme persistera; tu sentiras que la mort fait part des aventures promises et que l'immensité te porte et t'enveloppe mieux que le duvet du nid.*
>
> *Qui est celui-ci qui vient avec fracas par les rues désertes, et qui donne le repos dont la nuit était avare?*
> *Qui est ce buveur qui chante et vocifère? Sa voix enrouée vaut mieux que la guitare et le frisson qu'il donne est mieux que l'amour.*
> *Qui est ce vagabond qui rode et se lamente, qui frappe aux portes comme un créancier et un amant, comme un bourreau et un sauveur?*
> *Qui est cet envahisseur qui râle et qui exulte et délivre de tout, même de la liberté?*

You will wake up and search, and you will find no one. You will remember that you once could remember, but you will not be afraid. The words will be blotted out, but the rhythm will persist. You will know that death is one of the adventures that were promised to you, and that immensity bears you and enfolds you as softly as the down of a bird's nest.

Who is this who comes with clamour through the deserted streets, and grants the quiet of which night was chary?
Who is this toper who comes singing and shouting? His hoarse voice is sweeter than the lute, and the thrill which he gives is better than love.

Who is this vagabond who prowls about lamenting, who batters at the doors like a bailiff and a lover, like a tormentor and a deliverer?

Who is this invader who seems to triumph in his agony and sets us free from everything, even from liberty?

After this come a few passages of Racine. The first are from *Britannicus*. First of all the passage in which Nero tells how he suddenly falls in love, a passage which is as subtle in psychology as it is delicate in utterance:

> Cette nuit je l'ai vue arriver en ces lieux,
> Triste, levant au ciel ses yeux mouillés de larmes,
> Qui brillaient au travers des flambeaux et des armes;
> Belle sans ornement, dans le simple appareil
> D'une beauté qu'on vient d'arracher au sommeil.
> Que veux-tu? Je ne sais si cette négligence,
> Les ombres, les flambeaux, les cris et le silence,
> Et le farouche aspect de ses fiers ravisseurs,
> Relevaient de ses yeux les timides douceurs.
> Quoi qu'il en soit, ravi d'une si belle vue,
> J'ai voulu lui parler, et ma voix s'est perdue.
> Immobile, saisi d'un long étonnement,
> Je l'ai laissé passer dans son appartement.
> J'ai passé dans le mien. C'est là que, solitaire,
> De son image en vain j'ai voulu me distraire.
> Trop présente à mes yeux je croyais lui parler,
> J'aimais jusques aux pleurs que je faisais couler.

A few more lines from the same play:

> Princesse, en qui le ciel mit un esprit si doux,

and

> D'où vient qu'en m'écoutant, vox yeux, vos tristes yeux
> Avec de longs regards se tournent vers les cieux?

Some passages from *Bérénice*, the most "modern" of all Racine's plays. The story could be transferred into any time or place, and remain actual. This is not because it is ancient or modern, but because it is human, and therefore eternal.

> Soutiendrai-je ces yeux dont la douce langueur
> Sait si bien découvrir les chemins de mon cœur?

> Dans l'orient désert quel devint mon ennui!
> Je demeurai long-temps errant dans Césarée;
> Lieux charmants, où mon cœur vous avait adorée.

How heart-sick I became in the parched east!
I lingered wandering long in Caesarea;
Dear spots where once my heart had worshipped you.

Que vous dirai-je enfin? Je fuis des yeux distraits,
Qui me voyant toujours ne me voyaient jamais.

In short, from your unseeing eyes I flee,
That saw me all day long, yet saw not me.

And when the Emperor Titus protests to Bérénice that he loves her, although they must be parted for ever, she tells him that he need not protest so much,

Je vous croirais, Seigneur, sur un simple soupir.

The two most musical lines Racine ever wrote always seem to me two lines out of *Phèdre*:

Ariane ma sœur, de quel amour blessée
Vous mourûtes au bords où vous fûtes laissée.

It is said that when Rachel spoke these two lines on the stage for the first time the effect was so tremendous that Alfred de Musset fainted in his box. The effect was very great when Sarah Bernhardt used to say them. I once heard an extremely cosmopolitan critic, who disliked Racine, say that he thought the two circumflexed *u*'s were hideous; of course if that is your impression the lines would sound hideous, but those who admire these lines admire them because of the long repeated stress on the *u*, and the muted *e*'s at the end of the lines. Modern French poets have made great capital out of the long *u*'s. One poet (Arthur Rimbaud) went so far as to say that every vowel in French had a special colour; and that the letter *u* was green.*

But it is perhaps in *Andromaque* that Racine's verse reaches its high-water mark of freshness and purity. The verse in that play has the glory of the lilies of the field:

Captive, toujours triste, importune à moi-même,
Pouvez-vous souhaiter qu'Andromaque vous aime?

* "A noir, E blanc, I rouge, U vert, O bleu, voyelles."

or:

> Songe, songe, Céphise, à cette nuit cruelle,
> Qui fut pour tout un peuple une nuit éternelle,

or these, perhaps his most touching lines and (in the last two) a supreme example of under-statement:

> Fais connaître à mon fils les héros de sa race;
> Autant que tu pourras, conduis-le sur leur trace.
> Dis-lui par quels exploits leurs noms ont éclaté;
> Plustôt ce qu'ils ont fait, que ce qu'ils ont été.
> Parle-lui tous les jours des vertus de son père;
> Et, quelquefois aussi, parle-lui de sa mère.

What has always seemed to me one of the most poignant lines in poetry comes from *Mithridate*:

> *Mais la mort fuit encor sa grande âme trompée,*

which might be translated

> But Death still shuns his great defrauded soul.

The line sums up the whole lives of many great men who have outlived their prime and experienced disappointment, disillusion and ingratitude in their old age. A good example is Herzen, the Russian Socialist reformer, who lived to see his work misunderstood and "twisted by knaves to make a trap for fools". It might apply to Racine himself; or among younger men, that is to say among the middle-aged, to the Black Prince, pining away and sick of mortal disease at Bordeaux.

Next in my luggage after fragments of Racine there comes a long piece of Ruskin, about praising the young. It is a passage that all old people and all parents should read. But besides being a valuable sermon, it is extremely beautiful.

> For it is only the young who can receive much reward from men's praise; the old, when they are great, get too far beyond and above you to care what you think of them.
>
> You may urge them then with sympathy, and surround them with acclamation, but they will doubt your pleasure and despise your praise. You might have cheered them in their race through the asphodel meadows of their youth; you might have brought the proud, bright scarlet into their faces, if you had but cried once to them "Well done", as they dashed up to the first goal of their early ambition. But now their pleasure is in memory, and their ambition is in Heaven. They can be kind to you, but you nevermore can be kind to them. You may be fed with the fruit and fulness of their old age, but you were as the nipping blight to them in their blossoming, and your praise is only as the warm winds of autumn to the dying branches.
>
> There is one thought still, the saddest of all, bearing on this withholding of early help. It is possible, in some noble natures, that the warmth and the affections of childhood may remain, unchilled, though unanswered, and that the old man's heart may still be capable of gladness, when the long-withheld sympathy is given at last. But in these noble natures it nearly always happens that the chief motive of earthly ambition has not been to give delight to themselves, but to their parents. Every noble youth looks back, as to the chiefest joy which this world's honour ever gave him, to the moment when first he saw his father's eyes flash with pride, and his mother turn away her head, lest he should take her tears for tears of sorrow. Even the lover's joy, when some worthiness of his is acknowledged before his mistress, is not so great

[117]

as that, for it is not so pure—the desire to exalt himself
in her eyes mixes with that of giving her delight; but he
does not need to exalt himself in his parents' eyes: it is
with the pure hope of giving them pleasure that he comes
to tell them what he has done, or what has been said of
him; and therefore he has a purer pleasure of his own.
And this purest and best of rewards you keep from him
if you can: you feed him in his tender youth with ashes
and dishonour; and then you come to him, obsequious,
but too late, with your sharp laurel crown, the dew all
dried from its leaves; and you thrust it into his languid
hand, and he looks at you wistfully. What shall he do
with it? What can he do, but go and lay it on his mother's
grave?

Ruskin, *A Joy for Ever*.

Next comes a description of John Addington Symonds'
conversation written by Robert Louis Stevenson. It is called
Opalstein.

> He sings the praises of the earth and the arts, flowers
> and jewels, wine and music, in a moonlight serenading
> manner, as to the light guitar; even wisdom comes from
> his tongue like singing; no one is, indeed, more tuneful
> in the upper notes. But even while he sings the song of
> the Sirens he still hearkens to the barking of the Sphinx.
> Jarring Byronic notes interrupt the flow of his Horatian
> humours. His mirth has something of the tragedy of the
> world for its perpetual background; and he feasts like
> Don Giovanni to a double orchestra, one lightly sounding
> for the dance, one pealing Beethoven in the distance.

The last two passages were read and copied out in Paris in 1899, while the Dreyfus case was in full swing, and so it is not astonishing to find among them the following passage about courts-martial from Boswell's *Johnson*.

> Talking of a court-martial that was sitting upon a very momentous public occasion, he expressed much doubt of an enlightened decision; and said that perhaps there was not a member of it who in the whole course of his life had ever spent an hour by himself in balancing probabilities.

Then come some fragments from George Eliot—a serious sentence from *Felix Holt*:

> There is heroism even in the circles of hell for fellow-sinners, who cling to each other in the fiery whirlwind and never recriminate.

That George Eliot should have combined in her spirit such portentous solemnity and so fresh a sense of humour is a puzzle. Nothing could be more lively and more funny, and at the same time more true to life, than her comic characters. When Mrs Poyser says, "You're mighty fond o' Craig; but for my part, I think he's welly like a cock as thinks the sun's rose o' purpose to hear him crow", she says in a few words what it took Edmond Rostand four acts of verse to say in his play *Chantecler*.

Here is another of Mrs Poyser's sayings: "I'm not denyin' the women are foolish: God Almighty made 'em to match the men."

This reminds me of a remark I once heard a Russian lady make to someone who said a clever man had married a stupid wife: "Il faut être remarquablement bête pour être trop bête pour un homme." This same lady said to me, at the moment when the literary were having the time of their life casting the Victorians from their pedestals: "All the same, the people who admired George Eliot were not idiots."

They were not idiots, and they admired George Eliot greatly. F. W. Cornish, Vice-Provost of Eton, was not an idiot, and he enjoyed George Eliot. So did Augustine Birrell, and Mr Asquith.

It is difficult to give younger people of the present day any idea of the extent and intensity of George Eliot's fame and popularity. I am not speaking of the time when her books first came out, and surprised the world; I am not old enough to remember that; but I am speaking of a period as long after their appearance as the end of the 'eighties.

George Eliot's reputation and popularity, unlike George Meredith's, were neither confined to the intellectuals and the serious, nor eschewed by them. Her books were immensely popular with the public, and yet commanded the approval of everything that was most intellectual in England.

In 1885 I was at school at Eastbourne. There was at that time a popular reciter called Clifford Harrison, who gave recitals of poetry and prose. He gave these sitting at a grand pianoforte, and when the subjects were serious—and they ranged from Shelley to Bret Harte—he accompanied himself. When the subjects came under the heading of Comedy, he dispensed with the piano and acted the poem or the passage.

I remember attending one of these recitals, which was held before a packed audience, in what I think was called The Devonshire Park Theatre. The most popular item in the programme, the recitation which "got across" most indubitably, was a chapter from George Eliot's *Adam Bede*, called "Mrs Poyser has her say out".

I heard this same chapter read aloud a year or two ago, by a master of reading, and I thought that it had lost none of its freshness and humour; and I wonder it has not been seized upon by broadcasters. Of course it needs good reading; but then, so does anything.

Another example: I remember, when I was at school, saying to one of the more cultivated Eton masters what fun it would be if a really great writer were to appear on the scene, and he said: "You mean, someone like George Eliot?" And I said hopefully, "Yes, another George Eliot." Yet at that very moment Kipling's *Plain Tales from the Hills* and his *Soldiers Three* and some, if not all, of the little grey paper books first published in India were on sale. The great writer was there. It would be untrue to say that nobody suspected the fact. His fame came in a day, his books were snatched at and devoured greedily and praised by the most important critics (Henry James, Andrew Lang, Edmund Gosse, etc.). But at that moment people had no idea what an echoing reverberation his fame would make in the world, nor what was to be the world-wide range of his reputation, nor that he would one day be buried in Poets' Corner at Westminster Abbey, with a Prime Minister, an Admiral of the Fleet, and the Chief of the Imperial General Staff for pall-bearers.

We have no longer any patience with the ponderous scientific side of George Eliot. We* can no longer read *Romola*. But if

* I mean by "we" those of us, old or young, who can still read and admire George Eliot. Lord David Cecil, for instance. See his *Victorian Novelists*. Since writing this I have read *Romola* with pleasure and admiration.

one re-reads her fresh early books—*Adam Bede, The Mill on the Floss, Silas Marner,* and, among the later, great *Middlemarch* —they seem to me to put in the shade all more modern presentations of English middle- and lower-class country life and the peasantry. They seem to me to put them in the shade as much as a picture by Hogarth or Franz Hals annihilates certain modern pictures. Take her country characters, her lawyers, her auctioneers, her doctors, her farmers, her tradesmen, her yokels. They are presented in the round, they are as alive as the personages in Shakespeare's comedies; and what a world of characters she creates—what a large and detailed and crowded canvas!

When people say George Eliot's work is quite dead, and nobody reads her, it would be more accurate to say that her work is despised by a handful of intellectuals, and unread by several thousands of people after a certain age. But in spite of that, cheap editions of her books still have a permanent sale, and she is just as much admired in France as ever she was. One day I was talking to a French writer, and bewailing the fact that French criticism was hard and severe on certain authors who had written beautiful prose, on Maupassant for instance, and I quoted him a sentence. He admitted the sentence was a good one, and said: "Heureusement il y a l'étranger"—meaning that foreign opinion is sometimes a wholesome check on the vagaries, loves and hates, of temporary and local fashion.

Two years ago I had to visit a rough-rider in a hospital who had had a motor accident. He wanted some books to read, and I took him some Nat Gould, some Edgar Wallace, and a few other books of the same kind, among them a cheap edition of *The Mill on the Floss* which happened to be in the shop. When I visited him a little later he told me the book he had enjoyed far the most of my selection—and he had read them all—was *The Mill on the Floss.*

It is certainly a fact that, if you go to a bookshop in any of the provincial towns of England and Scotland, you will be able to buy some books by George Eliot in cheap editions, but you will not find Marcel Proust in any edition whatsoever. Marcel Proust was one of George Eliot's greatest admirers.

Interspersed with Dante, Donne, Racine, Tacitus, and others, there are many fragments of Ernest Renan.

At Mr Scoones' establishment, where I was prepared for an examination on and off for nine years, and where he himself lectured on French, he advised us to read Sainte-Beuve and Renan to improve our style, but he told us to read more of Sainte-Beuve than of Renan, for, he said, "Renan is sometimes stodgy and sticky." Maybe; but sometimes he isn't. One day Taine took a page of Renan and held it up to the window against the light, saying, "On ne voit pas avec quoi c'est fait." Among the great number of rags and tags of Renan in my luggage, there are four passages which have become part of the permanent furniture of my mind. The first two are about the religion of the Greeks:

> Un rien, un arbre, une fleur, un lézard, une tortue, provoquant le souvenir de mille métamorphoses chantées par les poètes; un filet d'eau, un petit creux dans le rocher, qu'on qualifie d'antre des nymphes: un puits avec une tasse sur la margelle, un pertuis de mer si étroit que les papillons le traversent et pourtant navigable aux plus grands vaisseaux, comme à Poros: des orangers, des cyprès dont l'ombre s'étend sur la mer, un petit bois de pins au milieu des rochers, suffisent en Grèce pour produire le contentement qu'éveille la beauté. Se promener dans les jardins pendant la nuit, écouter les cigales, s'asseoir au clair de lune en jouant de la flûte, aller boire de l'eau dans la montagne, apporter avec soi un petit pain, un poisson et un lécythe de vin qu'on boit en chantant; aux fêtes de famille, suspendre une couronne de feuillage au-dessus de la porte, aller avec des chapeaux de fleurs; les jours de fêtes publiques porter des thyrses garnis de feuillages; passer des journées à danser, à jouer avec des chèvres apprivoisées, voilà les plaisirs grecs, plaisirs d'une race pauvre, économe, éternellement jeune, habitant un pays charmant, trouvant son bien en elle-même et dans les dons que les Dieux lui ont faits.

Le Grec nous paraît toujours un peu sec et sans cœur....

> Nous autres, Celtes et Germains, la source de notre génie,
> c'est notre cœur. Au fond de nous et comme une fon-
> taine de fées, une fontaine claire, verte et profonde, où
> se reflète l'infini.

The next is the beginning of the famous prayer on the
Acropolis:

> Je suis né, déesse aux yeux bleus, de parents barbares,
> chez les Cimmériens bons et vertueux qui habitent au
> bord d'une mer sombre, hérissée de rochers, toujours
> battue par les orages. On y connaît à peine le soleil; les
> fleurs sont les mousses marines, les algues et les coquillages
> coloriés qu'on trouve au fond des baies solitaires. Les
> nuages y paraissent sans couleur, et la joie même y est un
> peu triste; mais des fontaines d'eau froide y sortent du
> rocher, et les yeux des jeunes filles y sont comme ces
> vertes fontaines où, sur des fonds d'herbes ondulées, se
> mire le ciel.

The fourth passage is about the early chapters of the Gospel of St Luke:

> ...on n'inventa jamais plus douce cantilène pour endormir les douleurs de la pauvre humanité.

The main fact about Renan as a stylist is that he wrote well because he had a lot to say, and wished to say it as clearly as possible. He used to keep a notebook by his bedside which he filled with notes in moments of sleeplessness. His methods as a writer are the exact contrary of those of a Flaubert or a Pater who spent days over a sentence, and hours over a word; and Renan's style is beautiful because there is in it a complete harmony between the thought and the expression: between *la forme et le fond*. In this he resembles Newman, who is a great stylist for the same reason. Renan and Newman both wrote a great quantity of books, and long books packed with knowledge.

Pater and Flaubert only wrote five or six books each, and that was enough to kill them. I am told that nobody reads Pater now, and even in the days of his popularity among the intellectuals, there were many people who could not abide his style—Samuel Butler, for instance. But surely his translations from the Greek are well written, and surely the sentence at the end of his essay on Leonardo da Vinci, talking of his death, is a good sentence. Here it is:

> We forget them in speculating how one who had always been so desirous of beauty, but desired it always in such precise and definite forms, as hands or flowers or hair, looked forward now into the vague land, and experienced the last curiosity.

To the young of my generation there was a certain excitement in reading Renan. We chuckled at his irony, thinking he had helped to emancipate us once and for all from many tedious superstitions, sham conventions, and false traditions. But his influence did not end there. It would have surprised Renan to hear that his histories of the origin and vicissitudes of the early Church, and his touching account of the laceration he suffered when he abandoned the thought of the priesthood and left the Church, should have been instrumental in bringing more than one agnostic into the Catholic Church. Such, however, is the truth. The reasons are briefly these. First of all, his histories of the early Church reveal to the agnostic who has had for sole religious education at school a certain amount of translating and construing of the New Testament, and some "talks" prior to confirmation, the astonishing fact that there was an early Church, of which the Apostles were the pillars; secondly, Renan informs them that his reasons for leaving the Church are not the so-called abuses of the Catholic Church, that is, the so-called "errors of Rome". For him, the Reformed Churches have not a leg to stand on. "Malheur au vague! mieux vaut le faux", he says. "I regretted at moments", he writes, "not being a protestant, so that I could continue to be a philosopher without ceasing to be a Christian. Then I realized that it was only the Catholics who were logical."

[127]   E*

Nor was it because he found it impossible to swallow Catholic dogmas.

His reasons, he tells us, were based entirely on philology and criticism; and had nothing to do with metaphysics, politics or morality. Such categories of ideas as the last-named seemed to him intangible and easily moulded to any shape. But the problem of deciding whether there were discrepancies between the fourth Gospel and the synoptic Gospels was entirely palpable. To him the evidence of such discrepancies was so conclusive that he was ready to stake his life on it, and consequently his immortal soul, without a moment's hesitation.

In such a problem there were none of those backgrounds which threw so much doubt on questions of politics and morals. He had no affection for Philip II or for Pius V: but had he no concrete reasons for disbelieving in Catholicism, neither the atrocities of Philip nor the fires of Pius V would have proved much of a stumbling block.

What drove him out of the Church was neither dogmatic difficulties nor the misdeeds of the Papacy, but his belief in the infallibility of the German higher criticism of the biblical texts.

"Ma foi a été détruite", he writes, "par la critique historique, non par la scolastique ni par la philosophie."

It was a real laceration. He is surprised at the levity with which others doff their faith. "En réalité," he said, "peu de personnes ont le droit de ne pas croire au christianisme. Si tous savaient combien le filet tissé par les théologiens est solide, comme il est difficile d'en rompre les mailles, quelle érudition on y a deployée, quelle habitude il faut pour dénouer tout cela!"

It was German textual criticism that cut the Gordian knot for him. He swallowed German criticism whole. He admired it, he says, all the more because he did not see limits to it. "L'esprit particulier de l'Allemagne, à la fin du dernier siècle et dans la première moitié de celui-ci, me frappa; je crus entrer dans un temple."

Renan probably never read the German higher criticism of Shakespeare, with a Shakespeare beside it in the original; but others did, and that shattered their faith once and for all in the

German higher criticism. Once one has read portions of that—however little one knows and whatever its merits may be—one can no longer believe German higher criticism to be infallible. For instance, if we read a scholarly and detailed argument written by a German, setting out to prove a possible thesis, say that *Richard III* was entirely the work of Marlowe, we may be duly impressed by the author's scholarship, ingenuity and labour, we may think he has made out a good case; there is much to be said on his side; but if at the same time we are personally convinced, after re-reading the play, that some passages have an authentic Shakespearean ring, and could not have been written by Marlowe, we do not on account of the thoroughness of German scholarship, learning and industry, renounce our opinion which we consider was based on common sense; we adhere to it. And after a course of the higher criticism of Shakespeare, we become aware that it is possible, as Father Knox has so brilliantly shown, to prove that *In Memoriam* was written by Queen Victoria; and when we see the German higher criticism at work upon the Gospels, and they tell us that certain of Our Lord's answers to Pontius Pilate are authentic, but that others are not, we merely reply, "Sez you!"

In taking as an example the theory that Marlowe wrote Shakespeare's *Richard III*, I am being ultra-fair to the German higher criticism; because many non-German Shakespearean critics and scholars have thought that parts of this play were written by Marlowe. Some have gone so far as to say that the whole play was written by Marlowe. Let the reader compare for himself the two following passages, and make up his mind if they are by the same man or by two separate authors. The first is a famous passage. It seems to me to have as Shakespearean a ring as anything Shakespeare ever wrote.

Clarence. Methought that I had broken from the Tower,
And was embark'd to cross to Burgundy;
And, in my company, my brother Gloucester;
Who from my cabin tempted me to walk
Upon the hatches: thence we look'd toward England,
And cited up a thousand fearful times,

[129]

During the wars of York and Lancaster
That had befall'n us. As we paced along
Upon the giddy footing of the hatches,
Methought that Gloucester stumbled; and, in falling,
Struck me, that thought to stay him, overboard,
Into the tumbling billows of the main,
Lord, Lord! methought, what pain it was to drown!
What dreadful noise of waters in mine ears!
What ugly sights of death within mine eyes!
Methought I saw a thousand fearful wrecks;
Ten thousand men that fishes gnaw'd upon;
Wedges of gold, great anchors, heaps of pearl,
Inestimable stones, unvalued jewels,
All scatter'd in the bottom of the sea:
Some lay in dead men's skulls; and, in those holes
Where eyes did once inhabit, there were crept,
As 'twere in scorn of eyes, reflecting gems,
Which woo'd the slimy bottom of the deep,
And mock'd the dead bones that lay scatter'd by.
 Brakenbury. Had you such leisure in the time of death
To gaze upon the secrets of the deep?
 Clar. Methought I had; and often did I strive
To yield the ghost: but still the envious flood
Kept in my soul, and would not let it forth
To seek the empty, vast and wandering air;
But smother'd it within my panting bulk,
Which almost burst to belch it in the sea.
 Brak. Awaked you not with this sore agony?
 Clar. O, no, my dream was lengthen'd after life;
O, then began the tempest to my soul,
Who pass'd, methought, the melancholy flood,
With that grim ferryman which poets write of,
Unto the kingdom of perpetual night.
The first that there did greet my stranger soul,
Was my great father-in-law, renowned Warwick;
Who cried aloud, "What scourge for perjury
Can this dark monarchy afford false Clarence?"
And so he vanish'd; then came wandering by

A shadow like an angel, with bright hair
Dabbled in blood; and he squeak'd* out aloud,
"Clarence is come; false, fleeting, perjured Clarence,
That stabb'd me in the field by Tewksbury;
Seize on him, Furies, take him to your torments!"
With that, methought, a legion of foul fiends
Environ'd me about, and howled in mine ears
Such hideous cries, that with the very noise
I trembling waked, and for a season after
Could not believe but that I was in hell,
Such terrible impression made the dream.

Richard III, Act I, Scene **4.**

Now compare this passage with the following lines from Marlowe's *Jew of Malta*:

But he whose steel-barred coffers are crammed full,
And all his lifetime hath been tired,
Wearying his fingers' ends with telling it,
Would in his age be loth to labour so,
And for a pound to sweat himself to death.
Give me the merchants of the Indian mines,
That trade in metal of the purest mould;
The wealthy Moor, that in the eastern rocks
Without control can pick his riches up,
And in his house heap pearls like pebble-stones,
Receive them free, and sell them by the weight;
Bags of fiery opals, sapphires, amethysts,
Jacinths, hard topaz, grass-green emeralds,
Beauteous rubies, sparkling diamonds,
And seld-seen costly stones of so great price,
As one of them indifferently rated,
And of a carat of this quantity,
May serve in peril of calamity
To ransom great kings from captivity.

* Modern commentators have altered *squeak'd* to *shriek'd*, but *squeak* was the word applied to the speech of ghosts in Shakespeare's time: witness his
     "Squeak'd and gibber'd in the streets of Rome."
Nobody would have dreamed of altering that *squeak'd* to *shriek'd*.

This is the ware wherein consists my wealth;
And thus methinks should men of judgment frame
Their means of traffic from the vulgar trade,
And as their wealth increases, so inclose
Infinite riches in a little room.
But now how stands the wind?
Into what corner peers my halcyon's bill?
Ha! To the east? yes: see, how stand the vanes?
East and by south: why then I hope my ships
I sent for Egypt and the bordering isles
Are gotten up by Nilus' winding banks;
Mine argosy from Alexandria,
Loaden with spice and silks, now under sail,
Are smoothly gliding down by Candy shore
To Malta, through our Mediterranean sea.

Jew of Malta, Act I.

In these lines the accent and tone seem to me those of another man's voice.

Before making up one's mind whether Shakespeare or Marlowe wrote *Richard III*, it is a good thing to taste a piece of undisputed Shakespeare, place it beside a piece of undisputed Marlowe, and compare the rhythm of both. Here is a passage from Marlowe:

But let me die, my love, yes, let me die;
With love and patience let your true love die;
Your grief and fury hurts my second life.
Yet let me kiss my lord before I die,
And let me die with kissing of my lord.

And here is Shakespeare:

I will instruct my sorrows to be proud;
For grief is proud and makes his owner stoop.
To me and to the state of my great grief
Let kings assemble; for my grief's so great,
That no supporter but the huge firm earth
Can hold it up: here I and sorrows sit;
Here is my throne, bid kings come bow to it.

[132]

Then there is the time factor to be considered. In France in the eighteenth century the partisans of Gluck used to come to blows with the partisans of Piccinni; and to the worshippers of each the music of the rival master seemed as different from that of their own idol as chalk is from cheese; but to us the music of Gluck is almost indistinguishable from that of Piccinni. In a hundred years time, or say two hundred years time, I think it may be difficult to distinguish between the verse of Byron, Shelley and Wordsworth, and I think that critics of the future might well go wrong in recognizing the authorship of the following stanzas; one is by Shelley, one by Wordsworth, and one by Byron:

> As some lone bird, without a mate,
> My weary heart is desolate;
> I look around, and cannot trace
> One friendly smile or welcome face,
> And ev'n in crowds am still alone,
> Because I cannot love but one.

> We meet not as we parted,
> We feel more than all may see,
> My bosom is heavy-hearted,
> And thine full of doubt for me.
> One moment has bound the free.

> Day and night my toils redouble,
> Never nearer to the goal;
> Night and day, I feel the trouble
> Of the Wanderer in my soul.

If Byron had thought there ever could be any danger of his verse being mistaken for Wordsworth's, he would have had a seizure. Shelley, on the other hand, would have been flattered. Wordsworth would have been sublimely incredulous.

The higher criticism might very well go wrong here; we know better now than to trust it entirely; but Renan belonged to an epoch when the German higher criticism was swallowed whole; and one cannot help thinking that had he been born fifty years later, or had the German higher criticism busied itself as

[133]

exhaustively with Racine and Molière as it did with Shakespeare, Renan would not have left the Church.

However that may be, he is partly responsible for the conversion of more than one agnostic, not only to belief from unbelief, but to belief in the Catholic Church; because his arguments lead to one conclusion, and to one conclusion only: namely, that if Christianity is true, and has not been proved false by the German higher criticism of biblical texts, then the Catholic Church is its only possible and logical manifestation on earth.

The view my generation took of Renan when they grew older is well voiced by Jules Lemaître, who in his youth was a fervent admirer, in the following passage:

> Le grand ouvrage de Renan, *Les Origines du Christianisme*, ces six gros volumes, où la moitié des phrases expriment des hypothèses et où l'autre moitié est ironique (et je ne parle pas de l'histoire d'Israël), cela n'est-il pas à la longue un peu décevant? (Heureusement, il y a ses essais, ses fantaisies, ses souvenirs, et sa *Réforme Intellectuelle et Morale.*)

The young generation in France detests, I am told, irony such as was practised by Renan, and more especially that of his disciple, Anatole France.

Side by side with Renan in my baggage there are fragments of
Keats, Victor Hugo, Leopardi, and D'Annunzio. The scraps of
Keats are from *Endymion*, which to me has always had the
fascination that early works of great writers have, before their
style is crystallized, before it becomes a definite style. Examples
of such works are Kipling's *Departmental Ditties*, and D'Annunzio's *Canto Nuovo*.

Here are some lines from Keats:

> Through the green evening quiet in the sun.

> Through buried paths where sleepy twilight dreams
> The summer time away.

>   as when heaved anew
> Old ocean rolls a lengthened wave to shore
> Down whose green back the short-lived foam, all hoar,
> Bursts gradual, with a wayward indolence.

>   gold-tinted like the peach
> Or ripe October's faded marigold.

> I loved her to the very white of truth.

> Æææ's isle was wondering at the moon.

> Sweet as a musk rose upon new-made hay.

> And as I sat, over the light blue hills,
> There came a noise of revellers!

Then, from one of Keats' letters, a line:

> An untumultuous fringe of silver foam,

and the end of the sonnet to Sleep:

> Save me from curious conscience, that still lords
> Its strength for darkness, burrowing like a mole;
> Turn the key deftly in the oilèd wards
> And seal the hushèd casket of my soul.

[135]

An Air, by Catullus, with a variation on the same theme, in English:

Lugete, o Veneres Cupidinesque,
Et quantum est hominum venustiorum.
Passer mortuus est meae puellae,
Passer, deliciae meae puellae,
Quem plus illa oculis suis amabat:
Nam mellitus erat suamque norat
Ipsam tam bene quam puella matrem,
Nec sese a gremio illius movebat,
Sed circumsiliens modo huc modo illuc
Ad solam dominam usque pipilabat.
Qui nunc it per iter tenebricosum
Illuc, unde negant redire quenquam.
At vobis male sit, malae tenebrae
Orci, quae omnia bella devoratis:
Tam bellum mihi passerum abstulistis.
Vae factum male! vae miselle passer,
Tua nunc opera meae puellae
Flendo turgiduli rubent ocelli.

Drop a tear and bow the head,
Leila's little bird is dead.
Hang a garland on the door,
Leila's bull-finch is no more.
He has gone where all things go
To the shadows and below
Where no seed nor gingerbread
Can recall him from the dead.
The plaintive pipe she'd rather hear
Than Philomel or Chanticleer
Is whistling now to phantom hosts
Of unresponsive hollow ghosts,
While he, poor bird, in shadowland
Hops upon no friendly hand.
Poor Leila! now he's gone away
She has not what withal to play!
Her bull-finch was her only joy;
She tires of every other toy.
The heart I gave her yesterday
Is broken too, and thrown away.

Of Victor Hugo I remember a great deal, but I have copied out little. The following dialogue, admired by Swinburne, from one of his least-known plays is an example of his descriptive powers at their best:

> *Otbert (lui montrant la fenêtre)*. Voyez ce beau soleil!
> *Regina.* Oui, le couchant s'enflamme.
> Nous sommes en automne et nous sommes au soir.
> Partout la feuille tombe et le bois devient noir.
> *Otbert.* Les feuilles renaîtront.
> *Regina.* Oui. (*Rêvant et regardant le ciel.*)
>   Vite! à tire d'ailes!—
> Oh! c'est triste de voir s'enfuir les hirondelles!—
> Elles s'en vont là-bas, vers le midi doré.
> *Otbert.* Elles reviendront.
> *Regina.*   Oui—mais moi je ne verrai
> Ni l'oiseau revenir ni la feuille renaître.

Victor Hugo's two greatest gifts were vision and pathos: and with the pathos, pity. Pity for those whom Dostoievski, a disciple of Victor Hugo, called the oppressed and the afflicted. His vision is of two kinds: he could have said, like Byron, "description is my forte"; he had a clear eye for describing things as they were, in the most striking and direct manner: *Choses vues*. Eckermann, when he was discussing Victor Hugo's verse with Goethe, praised the French poets for never abandoning the solid ground of reality: "you can translate", he said, "their poetry into prose."

Victor Hugo in his verse could tread firmly on the ground of reality. Nobody could evoke a clearer picture in fewer words —as in the passage I have just quoted, or sometimes in a single line:

> Le navire était noir, mais la voile était blanche.

But Victor Hugo could not only deal with the aspects of nature simply and directly: he found his way in the forests and on the mountain-tops of imagination. It is then we get descriptions such as the fight with the octopus in *Les Travailleurs de la Mer*, or stanzas such as the famous:

> Tout reposait dans Ur et dans Jérimadeth,
> Les astres émaillaient le ciel profond et sombre;
> Le croissant fin et clair parmi ces fleurs de l'ombre
> Brillait à l'occident, et Ruth se demandait,
>
> Immobile, ouvrant l'œil à moitié sous ses voiles,
> Quel dieu, quel moissonneur de l'éternel été
> Avait en s'en allant négligemment jeté
> Cette faucille d'or dans le champ des étoiles.

In reading verse like this we are conscious of something more than descriptive power and more than the choice of right words; an inner vision, a divine alchemy that touches words and changes them into more than mortal gold: a vision that does more than see things; that sees beyond and behind the meaning of things and peers into the secret workshop of God.

It is to this two-fold gift of vision, combined as it is with an unrivalled command and richness of vocabulary, an unsurpassed facility of rhyming and versification and verbal music, and the gift of pouring out great lines, to such pieces as the *Chanson d'Éviradnus* or to *Booz Endormi*, or to such single lines as:

> Les grands chars gémissants qui reviennent le soir

or

> Des avalanches d'or s'écroulent dans l'azur,

that Victor Hugo owes his place as the greatest French poet of the nineteenth century. Other poets of genius wrote poems and lines as beautiful as these from time to time, but Victor Hugo did it constantly. He did it constantly, and he did it so well that he swallowed up his own defects. His defects are easy to point out: over-emphasis, exaggeration, frequent lapses from the sublime to the ridiculous. Some critics have regretted that he survived the publication of his early books of lyrics. Verlaine, in an article on his death, says it is a pity he didn't die in 1844, and will not admit that he wrote more than one good lyric, *Gastibelza*: but Victor Hugo is a giant: his work is on the scale that transcends place and time. He is big enough to snap

[138]

his fingers, not only at the catchwords of schools, cliques and coteries, but at the shibboleths and the whirligig of literary fashion. His work has triumphantly survived the shifting moods of many epochs: three revolutions, an empire, and two great wars. A poet cares very little if he is abused by a small coterie of young men in an obscure café, when his work is read from China to Peru, and from the Indus to the Pole.

The changes of fashion matter little to one who appeals to the great public of many countries, because this public is serenely unconscious that such changes are taking place. They read to enjoy, and not because such and such an author is the fashion. Victor Hugo can afford to stumble, for he has strength in him to recover and gallop on for ever over the plains of time, as Belloc says about Shakespeare and Milton.

Then comes one poem by Leopardi:

Sempre caro mi fu quest' ermo colle,
E questa siepe, che da tanta parte
Dell' ultimo orizzonte il guardo esclude.
Ma sedendo e mirando, interminati
Spazi di là da quella, e sovrumani
Silenzi, e profondissima quiete
Io nel pensier mi fingo; ove per poco
Il cor non si spaura. E come il vento
Odo stormir tra queste piante, io quello
Infinito silenzio a questa voce
Vo comparando: e mi sovvien l' eterno
E le morte stagioni, e la presente
E viva, e il suon di lei. Così tra questa
Immensità s' annega il pensier mio:
E il naufragar m' è dolce in questo mare.

John Morley talks of "the crystal lustre of Leopardi's un-changeable despair".

In the year 1894 I wrote the following translation of the lines I have just quoted:

I always loved this solitary hill,
The hedge that from so many sides shuts out
The prospect of the sky's extremest line.
But I sit here and wonder, fashioning
With thoughtful fancy what may lie beyond:
Interminable wastes and silences
Tremendous and tranquillity profound,
Where for a while the heart roams unafraid.
And as I hear the wind blow through the leaves,
The silence infinite, the fitful sound,
Comparing, of eternity I dream,
Of seasons dead, of this one, of her voice.
Thus in immensity my thought is drowned,
And sweet to me is shipwreck in this ocean.

Then five lines from "the last song of Sappho":

> *Ecco di tante*
> *Sperate palme e dilettosi errori*
> *Il Tartaro m' avanza; e il prode ingegno*
> *Han la tenaria Diva,*
> *E l' atra notte e la silente riva.*

> Now of so many
> Once dreamt-of crowns and fond imaginings
> But Tartarus awaits me. My brave soul
> Surrenders to the Tænarian deity,
> To the dark night, and to the silent shore.

Leopardi calls this poem "the last song of Sappho", but the poem seems to be longer than any of the poems which Sappho has bequeathed to us; and those I have always thought are the best poems of either the ancient or the modern world. We do not know which was Sappho's last poem, but there is no sadder poem than the single line:

ἠράμαν μὲν ἔγω σέθεν, Ἄτθι, πάλαι πότα.

I loved thee once, Atthis, long ago.

As Swinburne takes six lines to translate these words, I will not quote his translation. It takes him six words to say "long ago", namely, "Long since in old time overpast". Yet his lines, to do him justice, do convey the spirit of the original.

I will quote instead eight lines written as it were to the tune of Sappho's lines, by Miss Elizabeth Belloc:

> Ah, once I loved thee, Atthis, long ago.
> The fields about the farm are silent now,
> Where in the windless evenings of the spring
> We heard Menalcas singing at the plough.

> Ah, once I loved thee, Atthis, long ago.
> I shall not see thy face nor touch thy hands.
> The empty house looks seaward: far away
> The loud seas echo on the level sands.

Of all the few fragments of Sappho that have come down to us, the most beautiful seems to me to be this one:

$$\delta\acute{\epsilon}\delta\upsilon\kappa\epsilon\ \mu\grave{\epsilon}\nu\ \grave{\alpha}\ \sigma\epsilon\lambda\acute{\alpha}\nu\nu\alpha$$
$$\kappa\alpha\grave{\iota}\ \pi\lambda\eta\ddot{\iota}\alpha\delta\epsilon\varsigma,\ \mu\acute{\epsilon}\sigma\alpha\iota\ \delta\acute{\epsilon}$$
$$\nu\acute{\upsilon}\kappa\tau\epsilon\varsigma,\ \pi\alpha\rho\grave{\alpha}\ \delta'\ \acute{\epsilon}\rho\chi\epsilon\tau'\ \acute{\omega}\rho\alpha,$$
$$\acute{\epsilon}\gamma\omega\ \delta\grave{\epsilon}\ \mu\acute{o}\nu\alpha\ \kappa\alpha\tau\epsilon\acute{\upsilon}\delta\omega,$$

translated as follows by the late Walter Headlam:

> The moon hath sunk, and the Pleiads,
>   And midnight is gone,
> And the hour is passing, passing,
>   And I lie alone.

Here is Miss Elizabeth Belloc's translation:

> The night is ebbing, and I lie alone.
> I hear the wind amid the orchard trees.
> I lie alone. Slow move the midnight hours.
> The moon is setting and the Pleiades.

In the spring of the year 1902 I was at Athens and was sitting one afternoon on the Acropolis, reading a book, when a Greek, a countryman dressed in skins, came up to me and asked me what I was reading. I happened to be reading Sappho's famous ode to Aphrodite, which was stuck into a small anthology I carried about in my pocket, just such a book as this one I am now compiling, only very much smaller and more compact. It had, in fact, been compiled on the supposition that we had the same or less of every poet than we have of Sappho: one complete poem, one almost complete poem, and a lot of fragmentary lines. The shepherd, or the countryman, whatever and whoever he was, took the book from my hand and, noticing the Greek characters, read out Sappho's ode from beginning to end, and, when he had finished, said it was country dialect, $\delta\iota\acute{\alpha}\lambda\epsilon\kappa\tau\sigma\varsigma$: *patois*.

The ode as read by him in his modern pronunciation and his country accent sounded incredibly beautiful, and from that moment, from the moment when I heard the rippling trilled dental R's and the musical vowels when he said the words

$$\chi\rho\acute{\upsilon}\sigma\iota\sigma\nu\ \mathring{\eta}\lambda\theta\epsilon\varsigma,$$

I have been convinced that the modern pronunciation of Greek is not fundamentally different from the pronunciation of the ancients. Certain vowel sounds may be different; but I am perfectly certain of one thing—that the Greek accents invented in later times to preserve the pronunciation do represent a subtle counterpoint between accent and quantity. I am perfectly certain the Greeks did not pronounce the lines of their poetry entirely according to quantity, any more than we do when we read the verse of Milton, or the French when they read Racine and Corneille. The quantity is there as a solid skeleton; the accent varies slightly with every line. The skill of the poet is his skill in counterpoint. I do not believe that the Greeks pronounced their language in the same manner as English or German schoolmasters, but perhaps a thousand years hence boys will be taught to read Racine like this:

Areéany masséwer dee kwél amoór blessée
Vouss moórutées awks boárds ow voúss futées lessée.

But that we English should still admire Greek and Latin poetry, although we pronounce it in a fashion which could but have distressed any ancient or modern Greek or any ancient or modern Roman is a mystery, and a testimony to the power of great verse.

There are two fragments of D'Annunzio—the first is from his earliest book of poems, the first stanza of a lyric:

O falce di luna calante
che brilli su l' acque deserte,
o falce d' argento, qual messe di sogni
ondeggia a 'l tuo mite chiarore qua giù!

O sickle of moonlight declining
reflected by desolate waters,
O sickle of silver, what dream-fashioned harvest
Is stirred by your gentle resplendence below.

And then two lines from one of his maturer works, which occur in the description of a warm autumn day in a wood:

Non so, quasi l' odore ed il pallore
Di qualche primavera dissepolta.

As if it were the odour and the pallor
Of some disburied, resurrected spring.

[143]

Then there comes a gap.

After I had shown the Customs House officer three trunks, one labelled "*Greek*, 1927–1928", one labelled "*Miscellaneous*, 1893–1899" and one labelled "*Dante*, 1893–1928", I came to another labelled "1916–1936", and I shall declare what I have got in it haphazard.

> A strong expression most he seem'd to affect,
> And here and there disclosed a brave neglect.
>
> Pope.
>
> In vain may heroes fight and patriots rave
> If secret gold creep on from knave to knave.
>
> *Id.*
>
> All sly slow things with circumspective eyes.
>
> *Id.*

Si un auteur n'était qu'un écrivain, Gautier serait un de nos plus grands auteurs, mais il ne faut jamais oublier qu'un auteur doit être un écrivain, et aussi autre chose.

Émile Faguet.

The greatest authors, besides being more than mere artists for art's sake, sometimes had definite professions besides literature, and were soldiers and adventurers, like Cervantes, actors like Shakespeare and Molière, intimately linked with human activities like Dante, diplomatists like Chaucer, civil servants like Milton. There are, of course, exceptions.

About Alfred de Musset:

> Avec un esprit très gai, il avait l'âme saignante et désolée;
> association moins rare qu'on ne pense.
>
> Barine.

This was true of Byron, and of Heine.

Things that involve a risk are like the Christian faith; they must be seen from the inside.

Henry James.

It is utterly futile to write about the Christian faith from the outside. A good example of this is the extremely conscientious novel by Mrs Humphry Ward called *Helbeck of Bannisdale*. It is a study of Catholicism from the outside, and the author has taken scrupulous pains to make it accurate, detailed and exhaustive. The only drawback is that, not being able to see the matter from the inside, she misses the whole point.

Des vers de haut vol, de ceux que le génie trouve et que
le talent ne fabrique jamais quelque peine qu'il y prenne.

Barine.

Such lines abound in Musset. For instance:

> la frileuse saison
> Sous ses grelots légers rit et voltige encore,
> Tandis que soulevant les voiles de l'aurore,
> Le Printemps inquiet paraît à l'horizon.

> Le soleil vient briser ses rayons sur leur cime
> Comme un soldat vaincu brise ses javelots.

> Les tièdes voluptés des nuits mélancoliques
> Sortaient autour de nous du calice des fleurs.

The remark applies equally well to Byron, Browning, Wordsworth, and many other poets.

A brain of feathers and a heart of lead.

Pope.

Druids and bards (their once loud harps unstrung),
And youths that died to be by poets sung.

Id.

Whether some brave young man's untimely fate
In words worth dying for he celebrate,

Cowley.

From La Fontaine:

> Le long d'un clair ruisseau buvait une colombe,
> Quand sur l'eau se penchant une fourmis y tombe.

> Un arc-en-ciel nué de cent sortes de soies.

> Guillot, le vrai Guillot, étendu sur l'herbette,
>   Dormoit alors profondément;
> Son chien dormoit aussi, comme aussi sa musette.

> Amour! Amour! quand tu nous tiens,
> On peut bien dire: adieu, prudence!

> Dans le cristal d'une fontaine
> Un cerf se mirant autrefois....

> Flore aux regards riants, aux charmantes manières.

> Ce n'est pas ce qu'on croit que d'entrer chez les dieux.

> Son art de plaire et de n'y penser pas.

That last line is the best description of La Fontaine, of himself and his work, ever made.

> Bref, se trouvant à tout et n'arrivant à rien.

> L'homme lettré se tut—il avait trop à dire.

There is a great deal of La Fontaine in my luggage; but the most valuable items are in my memory. I learnt some of the fables by heart before I was six years old. He was the bane of my childhood. He is far too difficult an author for the nursery or the schoolroom. A burden at school, where I had to "get him up" in examinations, and a source of boredom to my youth.

M. Hua, the French master at Eton, prophesied that by the time I was forty I should admire La Fontaine more than all the poets—and French poets were the only ones he admitted—and this came true. At the age of sixty I think he is the most perfect and unique of all French writers; and I would give "La Bourgogne et toute la Normandie, les tours de Notre-Dame, et le clocher de mon pays", as it says in the song, to have written such exquisite pictures of nature as:

Du palais d'un jeune Lapin
Dame Belette, un beau matin,
S'empara: c'est une rusée.
Le maître étant absent, ce lui fut chose aisée.
Elle porta chez lui ses pénates, un jour
Qu'il était allé faire à l'Aurore sa cour
Parmi le thym et la rosée.

Or

Un jour, dans son jardin il vit notre Écolier
Qui, grimpant sans égard sur un arbre fruitier,
Gâtait jusqu'aux boutons, douce et frêle espérance.

Or

A l'heure de l'affût, soit lorsque la lumière
Précipite ses traits dans l'humide séjour,
Soit lorsque le soleil rentre dans sa carrière,
Et que, n'étant plus nuit, il n'est pas encor jour,
Au bord de quelque bois sur un arbre je grimpe,
Et, nouveau Jupiter, du haut de cet Olympe,
Je foudroie, à discrétion,
Un lapin qui n'y pensait guère.
Je vois fuir aussitôt toute la nation
Des lapins, qui, sur la bruyère,
L'œil éveillé, l'oreille au guet,
S'égayaient, et de thym parfumaient leur banquet.

The lines about the twilight remind one of Gérard de Nerval's,
written to a Greek air and suggested by the modern Greek
words:

Νή καλιμέρα, νὴ ὥρα καλί.

Le matin n'est plus! le soir pas encore:
Pourtant de nos yeux l'éclair a pâli.

Νή καλιμέρα, νὴ ὥρα καλί.

Mais le soir vermeil ressemble à l'aurore,
Et la nuit, plus tard, amène l'oubli!

This reminds one of Byron's line:

The moon is up, and yet it is not night.

F

The whole of the *Fables* of La Fontaine the untranslatable, the inimitable, have been translated by Edward Marsh with admirable skill. He does the most difficult things best. Here are two examples, chosen from passages where La Fontaine is at his best:

> *Deux Pigeons s'aimaient d'amour tendre:*
> *L'un d'eux, s'ennuyant au logis,*
> *Fut assez fou pour entreprendre*
> *Un voyage en lointain pays.*
> *L'autre lui dit: "Qu'allez-vous faire?*
> *Voulez-vous quitter votre frère?*
> *L'absence est le plus grand des maux:*
> *Non pas pour vous, cruel!"*

> There were two pigeons on a tree,
> Who loved each other tenderly.
> One in his folly, tired of home,
> Resolved in distant lands to roam.
> "Alas, what ails you?" said the other,
> "You would not leave me, gentle brother?
> Sure, parting is the depth of woe,
> Although to you, unkind! it seems not so."

Krylov, the Russian fabulist, wrote a fable on the same theme, of which the first six lines are:

> Два голубя какъ два родные брата жили;
> Другъ безъ друга они не ѣли и не пили;
> Гдѣ видишь одного, другой ужъ, вѣрно, тамъ;
> И радость и печаль—все было пополамъ;
> Не видѣли они, какъ время пролетало;
> Бывало грустно имъ, а скучно не бывало,

which could be translated:

> Two pigeons lived like sons born of one mother.
> Neither would eat nor drink without the other;
> Where you see one, the other's surely near,
> And every joy they halved, and every tear;
> They heeded not at all how time flew by:
> Sadness they knew, but not satiety.

Here is the second example of Mr Marsh's skill. I have chosen
a passage of La Fontaine's graver mood:

> *La Mort avait raison. Je voudrais qu'à cet âge*
> *On sortît de la vie ainsi que d'un banquet,*
> *Remerciant son hôte, et qu'on fît son paquet;*
> *Car de combien peut-on retarder le voyage?*
> *Tu murmures, vieillard! Vois ces jeunes mourir,*
> > *Vois-les marcher, vois-les courir*
> *A des morts, il est vrai, glorieuses et belles,*
> *Mais sûres cependant, et quelquefois cruelles.*

> Here Death spoke true. When we are old as he*
> We should get up from life as from a feast,
> And take our leave as fits a thankful guest,
> Not clamour for reprieve that cannot be.
> Old Man, you murmur? Have you seen the young,
> How they walked steadfast, how they sprung
> To meet deaths proud and memorable, yes,
> But sure, and sometimes cruel, none the less?

> * "He" is the Old Man in the fable.

hogs
That bawl for freedom in their senseless mood,
And still revolt when Truth would set them free;
Licence they mean when they cry Liberty,
For who loves that must first be wise and good;
But from that mark how far they rove we see,
For all this waste of wealth and loss of blood.

Milton.

The most powerful men are not public men. The public man is responsible, and a responsible man is a slave. It is private life that governs the world. The world talks much of the powerful sovereigns and great ministers; and if being talked about made one powerful, they would be irresistible. But the fact is, the more you are talked about, the less powerful you are.

Lord Beaconsfield.

There is always something to worry you. It comes as regularly as the sunrise.

Id.

If you want to know what envy is, you should live among artists.

Id

Icare est cheut ici, le jeune audacieux,
Qui pour voler au ciel eut assez de courage:
Ici tomba son corps degarny de plumage,
Laissant tous braves cœurs de sa cheute envieux.

O bien-heureux travail d'un esprit glorieux,
Qui tire un si grand gain d'un si petit dommage!
O bien-heureux malheur plein de tant d'avantage,
Qu'il rende le vaincu des ans victorieux!

Un chemin si nouveau n'estonna sa jeunesse,
Le pouvoir lui faillit, mais non la hardiesse:
Il eut pour le brûler des astres le plus beau;

Il mourut poursuivant une haute advanture;
Le ciel fut son désir, la mer sa sépulture:
Est-il plus beau dessein ou plus riche tombeau?

Philippe Desportes.

Here fell the daring Icarus in his prime,
He who was brave enough to scale the skies;
And here bereft of plume his body lies,
Leaving the valiant envious of that climb.

O rare performance of a soul sublime,
That with small loss such great advantage buys!
Happy mishap! fraught with so rich a prize,
That bids the vanquished triumph over time.

So new a path his youth did not dismay,
His wings but not his noble heart said nay;
He had the glorious sun for funeral fire;

He died upon a high adventure bent;
The sea his grave, his goal the firmament,
Great is the tomb, but greater the desire.

I made this translation in 1918, and when it was published I
learned that the French sonnet was itself imitated from the
Italian of Sannazar:

Icaro cadde qui, queste onde il sanno, etc.

[156]

> Would I had given
> Both her white hands to death, bound and lock'd fast
> In her last winding sheet, when I gave thee
> But one—
>
> Webster, *The White Devil.*

How long have I beheld the devil in crystal!
Thou hast led me, like an heathen sacrifice,
With music, and with fatal yokes of flowers,
To my eternal ruin.

Webster, The White Devil.

These lines remind me of three lines of Musset:

Mais sa folie au front lui met une couronne,
A l'épaule une pourpre, et devant son chemin
La flûte et les flambeaux, comme au jeune Romain.

> Why should only I
> Of all the other princes of the world
> Be cas'd up, like a holy relic? I have youth
> And a little beauty.
>
> Webster, *Duchess of Malfi.*

"What wonders the poets effected by economy of phrase! He thought that phrase, 'a little beauty', gave a sharper, a more overwhelming impression of beauty—of rare and absolute beauty—than a thousand superlatives or than any array of sumptuous epithets."

Francis Bretherton, in *Cat's Cradle*.

And 'twere a comely music when in parts
One sung another's knell—

John Ford, *The Broken Heart*.

Sigh out a lamentable tale of things,
Done long ago, and ill done; and, when sighs
Are wearied, piece up what remains behind
With weeping eyes, and hearts that bleed to death;

John Ford, The Lover's Melancholy.

The first line and a half of this passage are put with supreme
appropriateness by Mr Kipling at the head of one of his stories—
Love o' Women: a story which some people consider to be first
among his masterpieces.

O, no more, no more, too late
   Sighs are spent; the burning tapers
Of a life as chaste as fate,
   Pure as are unwritten papers,
Are burnt out: no heat, no light
Now remains; 'tis ever night.

Love is dead; let lovers' eyes,
   Locked in endless dreams,
   Th' extreme of all extremes,
Ope no more, for now Love dies,
   Now Love dies,—implying
   Love's a martyr must be ever dying.
John Ford, The Broken Heart.

Parthenophil is lost, and I would see him;
For he is like to something I remember,
A great while since, a long, long time ago.
John Ford, The Lover's Melancholy

I but deceiv'd your eyes with antic gesture,
When one news straight comes huddling on another,
Of death! and death! and death! Still I danced forward;
But it struck home, and here, and in an instant.
Be such mere women, who with shrieks and outcries,
Can vow a present end to all their sorrows,
Yet live to court new pleasures, and outlive them:
They are the silent griefs which cut the heart strings;
Let me die smiling.

John Ford, The Broken Heart.

It is interesting to compare these passages from Ford with those from Webster. Ford seems to me to have a more melting simplicity. It is interesting to compare both of them with Shakespeare and with Marlowe. William Watson (an admirable critic in verse) once wrote an epigram called *After reading Marlowe's Tamburlaine*:

Your Marlowe's page I close, my Shakespeare's ope.
How welcome—after gong and cymbal's din—
The continuity, the long slow slope
And vast curves of the gradual violin!

This is true of the general impression received from reading Shakespeare after Marlowe, because Shakespeare's outlook is so far more sane and serene and less hectic and violent than Marlowe's; but so far as actual language goes, my experience is that foreigners find Marlowe much more easy to understand than Shakespeare. Of course there are moments in the Tragedies when Shakespeare achieves his most consummate effects by the simplest means, and by the use of the simplest words, sometimes indeed by sheer exclamations, like "O! o! o! o!" But if you read the bulk of Shakespeare, the language is not simple, and it may well have been as difficult to his contemporaries as it is to us, for he was the whole time inventing a language of his own. Phrases like

By the discandying of this pelleted storm

or

O answer me!
Let me not burst in ignorance; but tell

Why thy canonized bones, hearsèd in death,
Have burst their cerements; why the sepulchre
Wherein we saw thee quietly inurn'd
Hath oped his ponderous and marble jaws,
To cast thee up again

(although maybe they seem quite easy to us) are difficult to the
foreigner and complicated compared with Marlowe's phraseology
at his most frenzied moments. For instance:

Oh, thou art fairer than the evening air
Clad in the beauty of a thousand stars!

or

Tell Isabel the Queen I looked not thus,
When for her sake I ran at tilt in France,
And there unhorsed the Duke of Cleremont.

Or take the great single line:

See where Christ's blood streams in the firmament,

or the following fragment of dialogue from *Faustus*:

Faust. Tell me, where is the place that men call Hell?
Mephistopheles. Under the Heavens.
Faust. Ay, but whereabout?
Meph. Within the bowels of these elements,
Where we are tortured and remain for ever:
Hell hath no limits, nor is circumscribed
In one self place; for where we are is Hell,
And where Hell is there must we ever be:
And to conclude, when all the world dissolves,
And every creature shall be purified,
All places shall be Hell that is not Heaven.

The actual language, the diction, is a great deal simpler than
that of *Romeo and Juliet*, *Hamlet*, or *Macbeth*.

Er ist dumm wie alle Menschen, die kein Herz haben. Denn die Gedanken kommen nicht aus dem Kopfe, sondern aus dem Herzen.

Heine.

He is stupid, as all heartless men are stupid. Because thoughts do not come from the head, but from the heart.

Anatole France, in an early work, *Le Génie Latin*, writes as follows about Racine:

> Il était las; il ressentait cette amertume, ce grand mal de cœur, ce dégoût des choses qui vient aux meilleurs, à ceux qui travaillèrent avec le plus d'amour. Les hommes qui firent les œuvres les moins vaines sont ceux qui virent le mieux la vanité de toutes choses. Il faut payer par la tristesse, par la désolation, l'orgueil d'avoir pensé.

Again, he says of him:

> Cet art inné de prendre le tour de toutes les compagnies, le don de plaire, une souplesse délicate, une aptitude à toutes choses, faisaient de ce triste Janséniste un homme utile et l'engageaient dans mille intrigues plus avant qu'il n'aurait voulu.

About the first night of *Britannicus* he writes as follows:

> *Britannicus* parut l'année suivante (1669). Il n'y eut point de presse au parterre le jour de la première représentation, parce que, dans le même moment, on décapitait un homme en place de Grève. Le vieux Corneille était seul dans une loge.

Corneille disliked the new play, and Racine was intolerant of the older poet's criticism. This reminds one of Browning's lines:

> Like Verdi when, at his worst opera's end
> (The thing they gave at Florence,—what's its name?)
> While the mad houseful's plaudits near out-bang
> His orchestra of salt-box, tongs and bones,
> He looks through all the roaring and the wreaths
> Where sits Rossini patient in his stall.

Corneille sat impatient in his box, and Racine was impatient wherever he was sitting.

I stand like one
That long hath ta'en a sweet and golden dream.
I am angry with myself, now that I wake.

Webster, *Duchess of Malfi.*

And on the sudden, a clear light
Presented me a face folded in sorrow.
Webster, *Duchess of Malfi.*

J'aime mieux écrire beaucoup qu'écrire bien...enfin je n'aime pas corriger....Qui sait? Si au lieu d'écrire trente volumes j'en avais écrit trois, je serais peut-être un bon écrivain.

J'en doute du reste; et maintenant il est trop tard pour faire l'épreuve.

Émile Faguet.

I remember showing this passage to Arnold Bennett, who said he not only agreed with it, but that, applied to himself, it was perfectly true in every particular.

Self-confidence is the first requisite to great undertakings;
he indeed, who forms his opinion of himself in solitude,
without knowing the powers of other men, is very liable
to error, but it was the felicity of Pope to rate himself
at his real value.

Dr Johnson.

She, she is dead; she's dead; when thou know'st this,
Thou know'st how wan a ghost this our world is.

Donne, *First Anniversary*.

I copied this out on the day Sarah Bernhardt died, March 26th,
1923. Beethoven and Debussy both died on March 26th.

As much as in a hundred years she's dead
Yet is to-day the day on which she died.

D. G. Rossetti.

What have I done to you? Your deed or mine
Was it, this crowning me? I gave myself
No more a title to your homage, no,
Than church-flowers, born this season, write the words
In the saints' book that sanctified them first.
For such a flower, you plucked me; well, you erred—
Well, 'twas a weed; remove the eye-sore quick!
But should you not remember it has lain
Steep'd in the candles' glory, palely shrined,
Nearer God's Mother than most earthly things?
—That if't be faded, 'tis with prayer's sole breath—
That the one day it boasted was God's day?

Browning, Colombe's Birthday.

This is a good example of how sometimes in Browning a seemingly barren stretch of dialogue, narrative or disquisition will suddenly burst into flame. Here is another:

Like a god going through the woods, there stands
One mountain for a moment in the dusk,
Whole brotherhoods of cedars on its brow;
And you are ever by me while I gaze
—Are in my arms as now—as now—as now!
Some unsuspected isle in the far seas!
Some unsuspected isle in far-off seas!

Pippa Passes.

Someone wisely said that poets should be judged by their strongest links, and this is especially true of Browning. Sometimes in his chains the strongest link will come suddenly and unexpectedly. But sometimes, again, you will not be conscious of the links at all, but only of the strength of the chain when it is ended. I remember Vernon Lee saying to me once that in Browning's poem *A Grammarian's Funeral* every line was atrocious, an ear-sore, but the whole was magnificent. She said the same thing was true of Shelley's *Cloud*: nearly every line was bad, but the whole was incomparable.

Überhaupt ist die bedeutendste Epoche eines Individuums in der Entwickelung; später beginnt der Konflikt mit der Welt, und dieser hat nur insofern Interesse, als etwas dabei herauskommt.

Goethe.

As a general rule the most significant period in the life of an individual is that of his development. Later we have his conflict with the world, and that is interesting only in so far as it produces results.

That is to say, the history of the development of any young man is interesting; but the history of his subsequent life after he is fully grown up is only interesting in so far as it produces results.

The conflicts of Catullus and Heine with the world produced results.

*Es muß symbolisch sein—daß heißt: jede Handlung muß
an sich bedeutend sein und auf eine noch wichtigere
hinziehen. Der "Tartuffe" von Molière ist in dieser
Hinsicht ein großes Muster.*

Goethe.

Goethe says here that a play should be symbolic, that is to
say: each bit of action must be significant in itself, and point
to something still more important behind it. Molière's *Tartuffe*
is a great example of this. I think this is true of every successful
play, even in those plays in which there seems to be the least
action. It is true not only of *Tartuffe*, but of *Le Misanthrope*,
and of all Chehov's plays.

Lo, yonder inscription which blazes round the dome of the Temple, so great and glorious it looks, like heaven almost, and as if the words were written in stars it proclaims to all the world that this is Peter, and on this rock the Church shall be built against which Hell shall not prevail.

Thackeray, *The Newcomes*.

Those rare saints of God who rise up from time to time in the Catholic Church like angels in disguise.

Newman.

They are angels, but they are in disguise; and it has often struck me that one of the differences between the Catholic and the Anglican Church is this: in the Anglican Church personality is all-important: a clergyman attracts attention and commands a following by his personality, or even by his peculiarities; by being like a pillar box, as it were, if it were painted sky-blue.

In the Catholic Church a priest is like an ordinary pillar box, indistinguishable from a million others; but sometimes, owing to the sanctity of an individual priest, one of these pillar boxes will become as transparent as crystal, and the light within it will shine upon the world like the lamp of a lighthouse.

These are the angels in disguise that Newman talks of.

People complain of the scant evidence there is of Papal supremacy in the early days of Christianity; but Newman says: "It is a less difficulty that Papal Supremacy was not definitely formulated in the second century than that there was no formal acknowledgment on the part of the Church of the doctrine of the Holy Trinity till the fourth century. No doctrine is defined till it is violated."

Wissen Sie aber wie ich es mir denke?

*Der Mensch muß wieder ruinirt werden! Jeder außer-
ordentliche Mensch hat eine gewisse Sendung die er zu
vollführen berufen ist. Hat er sie vollbracht, so ist er auf
Erden in dieser Gestalt nicht weiter vonnöthen, und die
Vorsehung verwendet ihn wieder zu etwas anderem. Da
aber hernieden alles auf natürlichem Wege geschieht, so
stellen ihm die Dämonen ein Bein nach dem anderen bis
er zuletzt unterliegt. So ging es Napoleon und vielen
Anderen. Mozart starb in seinem sechs und dreißigsten
Jahre. Raphael in fast gleichem Alter—Byron nur um
weniges älter. Alle aber hatten ihre Mission auf das
vollkommeneste erfüllt, und es war wohl Zeit daß sie
gingen, damit auch anderen Leuten in dieser auf eine lange
Dauer berechneten Welt noch etwas zu thun übrig bliebe.*
(Goethe said this, talking to Eckermann.)

"Do you know how it appears to me?" he said.
"*A man must be broken up and scrapped.* Every extra-
ordinary man has a certain mission which he is called
to fulfil. As soon as he has fulfilled it, there is no more
use for him on earth and in his present shape, and
Providence will turn him to some other purpose. But as
everything here below goes a natural course, so will the
Daemons trip him up first on one leg and then on the other,
till he falls for good. Thus it happened to Napoleon and
to many others. Mozart died in his thirty-sixth year.
Raphael at about the same age. Byron when he was only
a little older. But each of them had completely fulfilled
his mission and it was time they should go, so that there
should be something left for others to do in a world
which has been planned to last a long time."

This is a satisfying thought, especially when one is inclined
to accuse Providence of waste, thinking of the multitude of
promising people who died young, and forgetting that part of
their very use, perhaps their whole point, was to die young,
and thus contribute in a unique manner to the symphony of
the universe.

I remember someone saying to me that one never came across an opinion of Goethe's without being struck by its essential wisdom, just as one never came across a sentence of certain politicians without being struck by its essential shoddiness and claptrap. His wisdom is so far-reaching and so manifold, his sense of proportion is so serenely satisfying, like that of the Pope he himself describes:

> *Der hohe Sinn des Papsts,*
> *Er sieht das Kleine klein; das Große groß.*

The lofty outlook of the Pope, who sees
The small, as small, and what is great, as great.

Sometimes he drops a piece of worldly wisdom like the following:

> *Ein Mächtiger, der für die Seinen nicht*
> *Zu sorgen weiß, wird von dem Volke selbst*
> *Getadelt.*

A man of power, who cannot look after the interests of his own favourites, will be blamed even by the populace.

Sometimes it is just the felicity of his utterance that renders it impressive; for instance:

> *Mit breiten Flügeln schwebte mir das Bild*
> *Des Todes vor den Augen.*

The image of Death soared before my eyes with outspread wings.

Sometimes a simple phrase reveals great depth of feeling—for instance:

> *Und so ist er mein Herr, und ich empfinde*
> *Den ganzen Umfang dieses großen Worts.*

And thus is he my lord; I apprehend
All that that mighty word encompasseth.

[179]

Or again:

> *Verlassen wirst du uns, es ist natürlich;*
> *Doch wie wir's tragen wollen weiß ich nicht.*

You will abandon us; well, very well;
But how we are to bear it, ask me not.

Here is an example of wisdom, originality and felicity combined:

> *Wir Menschen werden wunderbar geprüft,*
> *Wir könnten's nicht ertragen, hätt' uns nicht*
> *Den holden Leichtsinn die Natur verliehn.*

We mortals are most wonderfully tried,
Nor could we bear it, were we not vouchsafed
By Nature a divine frivolity.

The opposite of Goethe seems to be a man described by Saint-Simon:

> Son grand mérite étoit ses inepties, qu'on répétoit et qui néanmoins se trouvoient quelquefois exprimer quelque-chose.

Sometimes there is an outburst of fire, when one feels that Goethe is forgetting his Olympian calm, and uttering through the mouth of a puppet what he has deeply felt himself. For instance:

> *Frei will ich sein im Denken und im Dichten;*
> *Im Handeln schränkt die Welt genug uns ein.*

I will be free to think, and free to write:
The world prevents us well enough from doing.

Sometimes he breathes a sigh of infinite melancholy: for instance:

> *Ja, ich will weg, allein nicht wie ihr wollt,*
> *Ich will hinweg, und weiter als ihr denkt.*

Yes, I will go, but not the way you wish,
I will be gone, and farther than you dream.

This reminds me of Dryden:

> For I have far to go, if death be far,
> And never must return.

Sometimes there is a Sophoclean touch:

> *Ich fühl', ich fühl' es wohl, die große Kunst,*
> *Die jeden nährt, die den gesunden Geist*
> *Stärkt und erquickt, wird mich zu Grunde richten.*

> I know, I know full well, that Art, the mighty,
> That feeds all men, that to the healthy soul
> Gives strength and life, will bring me to my ruin.

Goethe's soul was too healthy to be shattered by Art, but he was aware that in him there were two souls, one, if it had not been restrained, controlled, and counter-balanced by the other, might well have led him to final ruin.

This point, namely the dual character in Goethe's nature that is expressed in *Tasso*, was pointed out to me in an extremely subtle manner by a Russian friend of mine who is now dead. I will not give his name, as he once told me he preferred to be quoted anonymously. He wrote to me as follows on April 15th, 1924:

"I have just finished *Tasso*—at your behest. The first bird's-eye view—a rather tedious puppet-play, with a lap-dog for hero: coming nearer so as to hear the words, you notice they are by no less a man than Goethe. Still nearer—you recognize the wires are pulled by the same. Nearer yet, the three male parts cut out from living flesh —Goethe's flesh. Last of all, you put together the three little pieces: Goethe's flesh—Tasso, Goethe's bone— Antonio, Goethe's distant mind—the Duke, and you have Goethe himself and a masterpiece fit to rank with *Misanthrope* and *Mariage de Figaro*. But I am far too stupid to see such things unless shown (want a Baedeker) and only notice the flesh is too raw and palpitating, the bone too dry, and the mind too distant: give me Molière and Beaumarchais where the harmony *saute aux yeux*

[181]

and the figures and details are graceful and amusing and no *Schönseelerei*.

> et me laissez enfin
> Dans ce petit coin sombre avec mon noir chagrin.

No stilts—just like Mozart; and Tasso is Beethoven. The quotation is from the *Misanthrope*."

How different is this criticism from a sentence I read lately in one of the daily newspapers, in which a critic said that Goethe was with difficulty "surviving over-estimation"; that the first part of Goethe's *Faust* was unreadable and the second was never read.

I have often heard it said that it would be well worth while to go through the drudgery of learning German solely to be able to read *Faust* in the original, and half a dozen other lyrics besides. It is not such lines as those which I have noted and quoted here, beautiful as they are, that put Goethe among the greatest poets. He does better still, in certain passages and phrases of *Faust*, and in certain lyrics. He said himself that all poetry should be occasional, and his own best poetry was occasional, whether he wrote it at the age of eighteen or eighty. But if a poet's work is entirely occasional, one must not expect from him an organic perfect whole, such as *Oedipus Rex*, or *King Lear*, or *The Tempest*. This will account for the disappointment nearly everybody feels in reading *Faust* for the first time. They expect not only an organic whole, but a spiritual drama with a beginning, middle and end. They get a magnificent beginning; the problem, or rather the elements of the problem, are set before them; the chorus of the Angels, the Prologue in Heaven, the Devil's challenge to God that he will wrest from him a mortal soul, and the Devil's bargain with the man that if ever the man should bid the fleeting moment abide, for it is beautiful, he must give up his soul. We expect to see this worked out, but all we get after the first part, after the elements of the problem have been stated, is a fragment: the story of the love and death of Gretchen. Goethe called the first part of *Faust* a fragment when it was originally published. A fragment it remained. It is true he worked out the problem and gave it a close in the second part, but the second part is less organic than the first, and is really a series of occasional fragments. In spite of this, the fragment of the first part of *Faust* and about half a dozen short lyrics besides are of such profound and unique beauty that they put Goethe among the great poets of the world.

I will go farther, and say, it would be worth while to go to the trouble of learning German, not only to read the lyrics such as those in *Faust* and *Wilhelm Meister* in the original, but even to taste the magic of two lines such as Gretchen's

> *Denkt Ihr an mich ein Augenblickchen nur;*
> *Ich werde Zeit genug an Euch zu denken haben.*

Think of me for a little minute only;
I shall have time enough to think of you.

Or these, from the Dedication:

> *Sie hören nicht die folgenden Gesänge,*
> *Die Seelen, denen ich die ersten sang.*

They cannot hear the songs that followed after,
The souls for whom I first began to sing.

Vernon Lee once said to me in a letter: "Surely the excellence of all poetry—what puts Shelley above Keats, Goethe above Shelley (in his Lyrics), and English, German and Italian Poetry so incomparably above French—surely *the* great thing is the co-ordination into a total mood, as distinguished from the charm of detached metaphors or descriptions or verses. (Think of Baudelaire, who, instead of poetry, really wrote *des vers*.)"

A lot could be said about this. I could say a lot in violent disagreement about French poetry, and Baudelaire in particular. It is a notable fact that during my lifetime Baudelaire is the one poet whose fame has never suffered an eclipse among the literary. He has always been admired, in England as much as in France, imitated and translated by succeeding generations. I remember writing to Vernon Lee in answer that in my opinion the co-ordination into a total mood she spoke of was triumphantly achieved by Baudelaire in many a poem.

Vernon Lee complained that Baudelaire only wrote *des vers*:

G

verse. The French and the Persians and the Chinese, and I think the Greeks and the Romans, asked for nothing more from their poets; but they stipulated that the verse should be good. Horace said that bad verse was intolerable. Baudelaire never wrote bad verse. Here are two lines as a sample:

> Mon cœur, comme un tambour voilé,
> Va battant des marches funèbres.

If you want an example of his "co-ordination into a total mood" turn to his *Crépuscule du Matin*, to the description of the dawn in Paris. It is still more wonderful than his several sunset pieces. Here are two lines of it:

> L'aurore grelottante en robe rose et verte
> S'avançait lentement sur la Seine déserte.

These two lines as a description of the dawn are worthy to rank with Shakespeare's:

> But, look, the morn in russet mantle clad
> Walks o'er the dew of yon high eastern hill.

I discovered in some old dictionary that "russet" in older English and older country English meant grey as well as reddish. That accounts for Shakespeare calling choughs "russet-pated".

I disagree as much now as I used to with Vernon Lee about French verse and Baudelaire, but I have come to agree with what she says about Goethe, Shelley and Keats. When one is very young one prefers Shelley to Keats. Then one is inclined to put Keats far higher. Then, when one becomes very old, one may or may not once more prefer Shelley. Mr Buxton Forman, the great editor of Shelley, told me that when he re-read the whole of Shelley's works to compile his final edition (when he was between fifty and sixty) he admired Shelley more than he had done as a young man. Shelley and Keats both died young, they were both immature; but I think Shelley was ripening every day, and Keats was already over-ripe; witness his recast of *Hyperion*, which I am told modern critics admire more than all his works now. I should like to leave it on record that I do not, that I think the first version infinitely the better. I think Shelley had the mightier mind, and I think the last act of the

Cenci, and certain stanzas of *Adonais,* and certain single lines and images, show a greater degree of inspiration, and a mind that soared higher than that of Keats. I am not only speaking of the imaginative splendour of certain images, such as:

> Life, like a dome of many-coloured glass,
> Stains the white radiance of eternity,

or

> To that high capital where kingly Death
> Keeps his pale court in beauty and decay,

or

> Or on blind Homer's heart a wingèd thought,

but lines that have a Greek simplicity, such as:

> Ah! Woe is me! Winter is come and gone,
> But grief returns with the revolving year,

or these:

> within the orb itself,
> Pillowed upon its alabaster arms,
> Like to a child o'erwearied with sweet toil,
> On its own folded wings, and wavy hair,
> The Spirit of the Earth is laid asleep.

Or take, for instance, a passage of perfectly direct blank verse, which has no splendour, imagery or lusciousness, but just an Elizabethan directness, power and simplicity, followed by a lyric of which any of the Elizabethans might have been proud. It is what Beatrice Cenci says to her mother in prison when they are awaiting trial and death:

> What 'twas weak to do,
> 'Tis weaker to lament, once being done;
> Take cheer! The God who knew my wrong, and made
> Our speedy act the angel of his wrath,
> Seems, and but seems, to have abandoned us.
> Let us not think that we shall die for this.
> Brother, sit near me; give me your firm hand,
> You had a manly heart. Bear up! Bear up!
> O dearest Lady, put your gentle head

Upon my lap, and try to sleep awhile:
Your eyes look pale, hollow and overworn,
With heaviness of watching and slow grief.
Come, I will sing you some low, sleepy tune,
Not cheerful, nor yet sad; some dull old thing,
Some outworn and unused monotony,
Such as our country gossips sing and spin,
Till they almost forget they live: lie down!
So, that will do. Have I forgot the words?
Faith! They are sadder than I thought they were.

Song

False friend, wilt thou smile or weep
When my life is laid asleep?
Little cares for a smile or a tear,
The clay-cold corpse upon the bier!
    Farewell! Heigho!
There is a snake in thy smile, my dear;
And bitter poison within thy tear.

Sweet sleep, were death like to thee,
Or if thou couldst mortal be,
I would close these eyes of pain;
When to wake? Never again.
    O World! Farewell!
    Listen to the passing bell!
It says, thou and I must part,
With a light and a heavy heart.

If you compare this with Keats's efforts in *King Stephen*, or
Otho the Great, one cannot but recognize that Shelley's calibre
as a dramatist, or rather as a dramatic poet, is far the greater.

Here is a stanza that Shelley cut out of *The Recollection*
because he noticed that it repeated rhymes he had already used
in the same poem:

Were not the crocuses that grew
    Under that ilex tree
As beautiful in scent and hue
    As ever fed the bee?

One could make a small and exquisite anthology of stanzas which have been rejected or cancelled owing to the fastidiousness or the variability of poets. There would be two stanzas of Gray. The first is a stanza that he originally inserted immediately before the Epitaph of the *Elegy* and rejected because he thought it made the parenthesis too long:

> There scattered oft, the earliest of the year,
> By hands unseen are showers of violets found,
> The redbreast loves to build and warble there,
> And little footsteps lightly print the ground.

One sees his point about making the parenthesis too long, but why he cut out another stanza which completed the picture of a day with a description of the evening it is impossible to tell: it occurs in the second or third edition of the *Elegy*, and it has always struck me as being the most beautiful of all the stanzas:

> Him have we seen the greenwood side along,
> While o'er the heath we hied, our labours done,
> Oft as the woodlark piped her farewell song,
> With wistful eyes pursue the setting sun.

There are two lines which Gray did not reject, but which he made one day when he was out for a walk:

> There pipes the woodlark, and the song-thrush there
> Scatters her loose notes in the waste of air.

One day the Abbot of Solesmes and a monk of St Paul's went out to visit the tomb of the Scipios, when they were overtaken by the rain. They took shelter until the rain should be over. A poor old woman, who had also taken shelter in the same place, watched them respectfully while they prayed; nor did she interrupt them until they had finished the last words of the *Te Deum*. Then, turning to them, she said: *Signori, che bella parola. Domine in te speravi, non confundar in aeternum.* And after a salutation worthy of a noble lady, she placed her bundle on her head and went away.

L. Veuillot, *Le Parfum de Rome*.

It was during the present solemnity that, excited by the way she came out with a hundred stirred ideas about her wheeling through his mind, he was for the first time and most vividly visited by a perception that ended by becoming frequent with him—that of the perfect presence of mind, unconfused, unhurried by emotion, that any artistic performance requires and that all, whatever the instrument, require in exactly the same degree: the application, in other words, clear and calculated, crystal-firm as it were, of the idea conceived in the glow of experience, of suffering, of joy.

Henry James, *The Tragic Muse*.

This is borne out by the precept and example of all great artists in every walk of life, whether they be actors, jockeys, singers, poets, conductors, boxers, soldiers or sailors.

Her character was simply to hold you by the particular spell: any other—the good nature of home, the relation to her mother, her friends, her lovers, her debts, the practice of virtues or industries or vices—was not worth speaking of. There they were, fictions and shows; the representation was the deep substance.

Henry James, The Tragic Muse.

This might have been written about Sarah Bernhardt, Rachel, Duse, or any of the great actors or actresses.

It would be interesting to know how Henry James affects the present generation of readers. He was conscious himself of having piped to people who refused to dance, and mourned to the dry-eyed; and pointing to his collected works, he once said: "Look on my works, ye mighty, and despair." And yet the books in his earlier manner, such as *The Portrait of a Lady* and *Daisy Miller*, were so popular that they were almost best sellers, and no doubt they are the easiest to read; but I do not think they are his most valuable contributions to the art and literature of the world. I think his most valuable contributions are the stories and novels written in his maturer second manner, and even, if you have the patience to read them, of his third manner. These are undoubtedly marred by the habit of infinite parenthesis, the tremulous desire of saying everything, that he acquired by dictation. I have had the patience to read all his novels, even *The Golden Bowl*, which, though it defeated me twice, I have ended by reading three times. But it took a European war to make me do this, and I know somebody else who had exactly the same experience. Of course there are many people who prefer authors that can be read easily without its being necessary for Europe to be at war to make such a reading possible. But the reason why I think the books of Henry James's later manner are more interesting, if you have the patience to read them, is this. Other people have written narrative which is as good and as delicate as *The Portrait of a Lady*, and short stories as clear and as perfect and as touching as *Daisy Miller*; but no one has thrown such a sharp and serious searchlight on certain intricacies and entanglements of the human passions and the conflicts of mortal souls as Henry James has done in such books as *The Wings of a Dove* and *The Golden Bowl*, nor has anyone shown a more subtle divination of what is going on under the mask of convention, prosperity, fashion, and extravagance, than he has done in slighter stories such as *In the Cage*. In such works Henry James has done something that no one else has done. There have been critics—for instance, Mr H. G. Wells—who have said that the whole thing was not worth doing, that the spectacle of Henry James's works in his later manner was like a hippopotamus or a rhinoceros (I forget which) looking for a

pea. I do not feel this. I think that what makes Henry James's
later novels interesting, original and unique is that they show
and express his power of revealing and diagnosing and presenting
the play and counter-play of human passions and human passion
in the most unexpected surroundings, and beneath the most
conventional masks.

How good his similes are! and the incidental criticism and
observation in his novels; for instance:

> He dived once more into his story, and was drawn down,
> as by a siren's hand, to where, in the dim underworld of
> fiction, the great glazed tank of art, strange silent subjects
> float.
>
> *The Middle Years.*

How acute all his remarks on writing are:

> The historian, essentially, wants more documents than he
> can really use; the dramatist only wants more liberties
> than he can really take.
>
> Preface to *The Aspern Papers.*

Here is another example of his illustrative power:

> Her own confidence always stopped short of a certain
> point; a little curtain of reticence was always suspended
> between us. Sometimes it appeared to grow thinner and
> thinner, becoming almost transparent, and revealing the
> figures behind it. Sometimes it seemed to move and
> flutter in the murmur of our talk, as if in a moment it
> might drop away, or melt away into air. But it was a
> magical web; it played a hundred tormenting tricks, and
> year after year it hung in its place.
>
> *Martin Eustace.*

And here is a valuable passage on the past:

> I delight in a palpable imaginable *visitable* past—in the
> nearer distances and the clearer mysteries, the marks and
> signs of a world we may reach over to as by making a
> long arm we grasp an object at the end of our own table.
> The table is the one, the common expanse, and where we

[192]

lean, so stretching, we find it firm and continuous. That, to my imagination, is the past fragrant of all, or of almost all, the poetry of the thing outlived and lost and gone, and yet in which the precious element of closeness, telling so of connexions but tasting so of differences, remains appreciable.

Preface to The Aspern Papers.

There now comes in my luggage a whole tray of *Don Quixote*. Here is some of it.

> *Solo se vence la pasión amorosa con huída, y que nadie se ha de poner a brazos con tan poderoso enemigo, porque es menester fuerzas divinas para vencer las suyas humanas.*

Love is too strong to be overcome by anything except flight, nor ought mortal creature to be so presumptuous as to stand the encounter, since there is need of something more than human, and indeed heavenly, powers to vanquish human passion.

> *No hay libro tan malo que no tenga algo bueno.*

There is no book so bad but there is something good in it.

Don Quixote had the same opinion of actors as Hamlet, when Hamlet said they were the abstract and brief chronicles of the time. He calls them instruments of great good to the common weal, presenting us with a looking-glass at every step, in which we can see the vicissitudes of human life, and he remarks, "there is no representation which renders us more vividly as we are than comedy and comedians". Don Quixote said that you could survive anything except death, before the wits of the French eighteenth century, and the wits of the English 'nineties. Here is the sentence:

> *Todas las cosas tienen remedio sino es la muerte.*

There is a remedy to all things except to Death.

There is a fine passage about the theatre of life:

> *Pues lo mismo, dijo don Quijote, acontece en la comedia y trato deste mundo, donde unos hacen los emperadores, otros los pontifices, y finalmente todas cuantas figuras se pueden introducir en una comedia; pero en llegando al fin, que es cuando se acaba la vida, a todos les quita la muerte las ropas que los diferenciaban, y quedan iguales en la sepultura.*

"Why, the same thing", said Don Quixote, "happens in the comedy and theatre of this world, where some play the emperors, others the bishops, and, lastly, all the parts that may be in a comedy; but in the end—that is, the end of our life—death takes away all the robes that make them differ, and at their burial they are equal."

Shelton.

Then there is a beautiful sentence:

pero es tan grande como una lanza, y tan fresca como una mañana de abril.

For she is as tall as a lance, and as fresh as an April morning.

No book has such a good beginning as *Don Quixote*:

En un lugar de la Mancha, de cuyo nombre no quiero acordarme, no há mucho tiempo que vivia un hidalgo de los de lanza en astillero, adarga antigua, rocin flaco, y galgo corredor.

In a village of La Mancha, the name of which I purposely omit, there lived, not long ago, one of those gentlemen, who usually keep a lance upon a rack, an old target, a lean horse, and a greyhound for coursing.

Jarvis.

Another excellent beginning is that of Tolstoi's *Anna Karenina*:

All happy families resemble one another; every unhappy family is unhappy in its own way.

Everything had gone wrong in the house of the Oblonskys.

And another super-excellent beginning is that of *Hamlet*:

Elsinore. A platform before the castle.
FRANCISCO *at his post. Enter to him* BERNARDO.

Bernardo. Who's there?

No book has a finer end than *Don Quixote*, when the knight sends for his confessor and says:

Yo, señores, siento que me voy muriendo á toda priesa

[195]

déjense burlas aparte, y tráiganme un confesor que me confiese, y un escribano que haga mi testamento, que en tales trances como éste no se ha de burlar el hombre con el alma;

...Good Sirs, I perceive and feel death to follow me at my heels. Let us leave off and quit all merriments and jesting, and let me have a confessor to shrift me, and a notary to draw my last will and testament. In the extremity whereunto I now find and feel myself, a man must not make a jest of his soul....

Shelton.

Sainte-Beuve said that Napoleon as a writer was a master of words:

Napoléon écrivain est l'un des maîtres de la parole.

I have never come across a sentence quoted as having been said by Napoleon without wishing to copy it out. He says somewhere in his correspondence that the Italians are a race fundamentally inimical to the French—"un peuple foncière-ment ennemi des français, par préjugés, par l'habitude des siècles, par caractère".

One of the most interesting remarks I think he ever made is this one:

"Moi," disait-il à Roederer, "je n'ai pas d'ambition," puis se reprenant avec sa lucidité ordinaire, "ou si j'en ai elle m'est si naturelle, elle m'est tellement innée, elle est si bien attachée à mon existence qu'elle est comme le sang qui coule dans mes veines, comme l'air que je respire."

Taine, *Régime Moderne.*

At St Helena he said to Beauterne, "I know men, and I tell you that Jesus Christ was not a man."

In 1933 a book was published by M. Marquiset giving the shorthand report of what Napoleon said at the sessions of the Council of State held at the Tuileries in 1804–1805.

This is what he said one day about education. We have his very words:

On n'a vu jusqu'à présent de bons enseignements que dans les corps ecclésiastiques. Je préfère voir les enfants d'un village entre les mains d'un homme qui ne sait que son catéchisme et dont je connais les principes, que d'un quart de savant qui n'a point de base pour sa morale et point d'idée fixe. La religion est la vaccine de l'imagination, elle la préserve de toutes les croyances dangereuses et absurdes. Un frère ignorantin suffit de dire à l'homme du peuple: "Cette vie est un passage." Si vous ôtez la foi au peuple vous n'aurez que des voleurs de grand chemin.

[197]

This passage by nature of its prophetic quality is important enough to translate, lest it should escape the notice of some non-French scholar whom it might interest:

> Up to the present the only good education we have met with is that of the ecclesiastical bodies. I would rather see the children of a village in the hands of a man who only knows his catechism, but whose principles are known to me, than of a half-baked man of learning who has no foundations for his morality and no fixed ideas. Religion is the vaccine of the imagination, she preserves it from all dangerous and absurd beliefs. An Ignorantine friar knows enough to tell a working man that this life is but a passage. If you take faith away from the people you will end by producing nothing but highway robbers.

This has come true.

Side by side with Napoleon's comments on religion, I find a
religious poem by Skelton (1460?–1529):

Woffully araid

Woffully araid,
  My blode, man
  For thé ran,
It may not be naid;
  My body bloo and wan,
  Woffully araid.

Beholde me, I pray thé, with all thi hole reson,
And be not so hard hartid, and ffor this encheson,
Sith I for thi sowle sake was slayne in good seson,
Begylde and betraide by Judas fals treson;
  Unkyndly entretid,
  With sharpe corde sore fretid,
  The Jewis me thretid,
They mowid, they grynned, they scornyd me,
Condempnyd to deth, as thou maist se,
  Woffully araid.

Thus nakyd am I nailid, O man, for thy sake!
I loue thé, then loue me; why slepist thou? awake!
Remembir my tender hart rote for thé brake,
With panys my vaynys constreyned to crake;
  Thus toggid to and fro,
  Thus wrappid all in woo,
  Whereas neuer man was so,
Entretid thus in most cruel wyse,
Was like a lombe offerd in sacrifice,
  Woffully araid.

Of sharpe thorne I haue worne a crowne on my hede,
So paynyd, so straynyd, so rufull, so red;
Thus bobbid, thus robbid, thus for thy loue ded,
Onfaynyd not deynyd my blod for to shed;
  My fete and handes sore
  The sturdy nailis bore;
  What my3t I suffer more

Than I haue don, O man, for thé?
Cum when thou list, wellcum to me,
    Woffully araid.

Off record thy good Lord y haue beyn and schal bee;
I am thyn, thou artt myne, my brother y call thee;
Thé loue I enterly; see whatt ys befall me!
Sore bettyng, sore threytyng, to mak thee, man, all fre:
    Why art thou unkynde?
    Why hest nott mee yn mynde?
    Come ȝytt and thou schalt fynde
Myne endlys mercy and grace;
See how a spere my hert dyd race,
    Woffully araid.

Deyr brother, noo other thyng y off thee desyre
Butt gyue me thyne hert fre to rewarde myn hyre:
Y wrouȝt thé, I bowgȝt thé frome eternal fyre;
I pray thé aray thé tooward my hyȝt empyre,
    Aboue the oryent,
    Wheroff y am regent,
    Lord God omnypotent,
Wyth me too reyn yn endlys welthe;
Remember, man, thy sawlys helthe.

Wooffully araid,
    My blode, man
    For thé ran,
It may not be naid;
    My body bloo and wan,
Woofully araid.

A name that crops up frequently in my luggage between the years 1892 and 1928 is that of John Oliver Hobbes. For the moment her work has been forgotten, but I cannot help thinking that a time will come when some modern will have the great fun of rediscovering her. Rediscovered she is bound to be; for her work has an historical interest. It carries on the panorama of English country and county life which was begun by Miss Austen and carried on until the end of the 'seventies by Anthony Trollope. Up to the death of Trollope in the 'eighties we have a complete and continuous picture of English county society; but at Trollope's death we need somebody to carry it on. Who is there? Well, first of all there is Rhoda Broughton, who continues the picture until the 1900's, and whose work will be rediscovered for the same reason by those who will be curious to know what English county life was like during those years.

When I was a child, I remember Trollope still being talked about as a famous and popular writer. By the time I reached a public school his fame was eclipsed, and the young would not have dreamt of reading him. Since then he has been rediscovered, and the modern young say that he is the only Victorian they find completely satisfactory.

During the epoch of this rediscovery a lot has been written about him. Whether he is actually read as much by the moderns as they profess they read him, I do not know. I only know that whenever I have asked for a volume of Trollope at the London Library, I have never failed to get it, except once or twice when I have been told the book was being read by Mr Belloc, and he has told me that the only time that he has failed to get a Trollope from the London Library is when the book has been in my hands. However that may be, Trollope is the fashion, and he is unparalleled as an accurate chronicler of English county life and society.

When John Oliver Hobbes's work is rediscovered, people will be surprised at her wit. At the beginning of *The Sinner's Comedy* she describes the death of the ninth Lord Middlehurst thus:

> He did not speak again till just before he died, when he kissed his wife's hand with a singular tenderness, and

[201]

called her Elizabeth. She had been christened Augusta
Frederica, but then, as the doctors explained, dying men
often make these mistakes.

John Oliver Hobbes was naturally witty and had a brilliant
gift of epigram. Besides this, she could portray the ordinary
well-to-do county class with merciless observation and accuracy.
Here is a picture which combines all three gifts:

> Mrs Digby Vallence was tall and spare, with a small face,
> big eyes, and a large mouth. Digby was fond of saying
> that his wife's face was geometrically impossible. The
> parts were greater than the whole. She was a very amiable,
> intelligent woman, who played Schumann with a weak
> wrist, and was noted for her cooking recipes.
>
> *The Sinner's Comedy.*

Moreover, in rediscovering the work of John Oliver Hobbes,
the critics of the future will find that her work is a mine of
wisdom as well as of wit.

Here, for instance, is a piece of wisdom:

> A false success made by the good humour of outside
> influences is always peaceful; a real success made by the
> qualities of the thing itself is always a declaration of war.
> The man whom one praises with one's tongue in one's
> cheek is negligible; at any moment one can cease praising,
> and he must collapse. The man who continues whether
> he be praised or blamed is a mark for violent and un-
> reasoning animosity; not because he is hateful as an
> individual, but because he represents that something
> immortal and defiant which men fear in themselves, and
> call their own souls. It is for artists to remind humanity
> of the unconquerable and to assert the eternity of ideas.
> Stone the idealist—no flint can reach his thoughts. Bury
> the dreamer—his dreams will colour the sky above his
> grave. Slay the cunning player—his melodies will have
> mixed themselves with the air, and the winds which
> cannot be slain will sing out his music for ever from the
> tree-tops. Banish the prophet—his prophecies, never-

theless, will come to pass where he has uttered them. Imprison the philosopher—his philosophy will wander freely in the market-place. It is natural that brute force and brute anger should be roused to do their worst—at least, against the disobedient, inaccessible, and unseen agencies of the world; what is it but the larger spectacle of the strife, in each individual, between the flesh and the spirit? Men have passionate bodies; women have passionate souls; artists have passionate souls and bodies. No wonder they are misunderstood—or can it be that they are understood too well?

The Dream and the Business.

Here is a sentence which one of the women-characters says in the same book:

I have been thinking there are two kinds of men—those who were born to protect us, and those who were born to understand us.

Todos los contentos desta vida pasan como sombra y sueño,
ó se marchitan como la flor de campo.

Cervantes, *Don Quixote.*

All the joys of this life pass like a shadow and a dream,
or wither like the flower of the field.

There was a wonderful woman called Marie Lenéru. She was
blind, and a woman of the highest culture. She wrote this:

> Si nous sommes les maîtres de ce monde, nous en sommes
> aussi les hôtes. Les jeunes animaux m'inspirent toujours
> un mouvement d'hospitalité, les nouveaux domestiques
> aussi. Non seulement nous ne devons pas faire du mal
> aux êtres; mais nous devons les gâter, les conseiller.

I next come to the name of Maupassant, and I have often thought that a Frenchman could make a beautiful anthology of short passages of prose dealing with the French landscape, especially with the banks of the Seine and the fields of Normandy. Here are two glimpses: one is an autumn picture:

> Et sans cesse, tout le long du jour, comme une pluie incessante et triste à faire pleurer, ces dernières feuilles, toutes jaunes maintenant, pareilles à de larges sous d'or, se détachaient, tournoyaient, voltigeaient et tombaient.

A winter landscape:

> Un rideau de flocons blancs ininterrompu miroitait sans cesse en descendant vers la terre; il effaçait les formes, poudrait les choses d'une mousse de glace; et l'on n'entendait plus dans le grand silence de la ville calme et ensevelie sous l'hiver que ce froissement vague, innommable et flottant de la neige qui tombe, plutôt sensation que bruit, entremêlement d'atomes légers qui semblaient emplir l'espace, couvrir le monde.

This sentence, which seems to me one of the most perfect ever written, has always reminded me of some lines of Robert Bridges on London snow:

> When men were all asleep the snow came flying,
> In large white flakes falling on the city brown,
> Stealthily and perpetually settling and loosely lying,

and of this sentence of Coleridge:

> His life was playful from infancy to death, like the snow which in a calm day falls, but scarce seems to fall, and plays and dances in and out till the very moment that it gently reaches the earth.

The writers who have painted English landscape as well as Maupassant painted French landscape seem to me to be Crabbe, Tennyson, and Robert Bridges. Crabbe gives you a landscape in a line. For instance:

Ships softly sinking in the sleepy sea,

or, again, the three following autumn pieces:

Before him swallows gathering for the sea
Took their short flights and twitter'd on the lea;
And near the bean-sheaf stood, the harvest done,
And slowly blacken'd in the sickly sun.

There was a day, ere yet the autumn closed,
When, ere her wintry wars, the earth reposed,
When from the yellow weed the feathery crown,
Light as the curling smoke, fell slowly down;
When the winged insect settled in our sight,
And waited wind to recommence her flight;
When the wide river was a silver sheet,
And on the ocean slept th' unanchor'd fleet.

It was a fair and mild autumnal sky,
And earth's ripe treasures met th' admiring eye,
As a rich beauty, when her bloom is lost,
Appears with more magnificence and cost:
The wet and heavy grass, where feet had stray'd,
Not yet erect, the wanderer's way betray'd;
Showers of the night had swell'd the deep'ning rill,
The morning breeze had urged the quick'ning mill;
Assembled rooks had wing'd their sea-ward flight,
By the same passage to return at night,
While proudly o'er them hung the steady kite,
Then turn'd him back, and left the noisy throng,
Nor deign'd to know them as he sail'd along.
Long yellow leaves, from oziers, strew'd around,
Choked the small stream, and hush'd the feeble sound;
While the dead foliage dropt from loftier trees
Our squire beheld not with his wonted ease,
But to his own reflections made reply,
And said aloud: "Yes! doubtless we must die."

[207]

Here is an example of Tennyson's landscape painting:

> The great waters break
> Whitening for half a league and thin themselves,
> Far over sands marbled with moon and cloud.

Swinburne quotes as a triumph of evocation and accurate observation the line (describing the east coast of England):

> And white ships flying on the yellow sea.

Pushkin achieves a still more vivid effect, without using any adjectives, in the following lines:

> и царь
> Могъ съ вышины съ весельемъ озирать
> И долъ, покрытый бѣлыми шатрами,
> И море, гдѣ бѣжали корабли,

which I have translated thus:

> And the King
> Could from that summit joyfully survey
> The plain bestrewn with white pavilions,
> And ships with flying sail upon the sea.

But where the consummate art of Tennyson's interpretation of the English landscape is seen at its best is in *In Memoriam*. For instance, this description of a summer dawn:

> Till now the doubtful dusk reveal'd
>   The knolls once more where, couch'd at ease,
>   The white kine glimmer'd, and the trees
> Laid their dark arms about the field;
>
> And suck'd from out the distant gloom
>   A breeze began to tremble o'er
>   The large leaves of the sycamore,
> And fluctuate all the still perfume;
>
> And gathering freshlier overhead,
>   Rock'd the full-foliaged elms, and swung
>   The heavy-folded rose, and flung
> The lilies to and fro, and said

[208]

"The dawn, the dawn," and died away,
   And East and West, without a breath,
   Mixt their dim lights, like life and death,
To broaden into boundless day.

Those people who think that the plays of Shakespeare were not written by William Shakespeare of Stratford on Avon, but by someone else, are nevertheless constrained to face the fact that they were written by a man who had an intimate knowledge of the country and the field sports of his day. Take the following passage, for instance, from *Henry IV* (Part I), Act ɪᴠ, Scene 1:

> All furnisht, all in Armes,
> All plum'd like Estridges, that with the Winde
> Bayted like Eagles, having lately bath'd,
> Glittering in Golden Coates like Images,
> As full of spirit as the Moneth of May,
> And gorgeous as the Sunne at Mid-summer,
> Wanton as youthfull Goates, wilde as young Bulls.
> I saw young *Harry* with his Bever on,
> His Cushes on his thighes, gallantly arm'd,
> Rise from the ground like feathered *Mercury*,
> And vaulted with such ease into his Seat,
> As if an Angell dropt downe from the Clouds,
> To turne and winde a fierie Pegasus,
> And witch the World with Noble Horsemanship.

This passage, in which I have followed the text of the First Folio, has given rise to an interesting controversy, turning on two points: (1) whether by "estridges" Shakespeare meant ostriches or goshawks, (2) whether the reading in the second line should be "'with the wind" or "wing the wind". D. H. Madden, in his book *The Diary of Master William Silence*, which is an exhaustive study of Shakespeare and of Elizabethan sport, comments as follows on the passage:

> Thus Shakespeare wrote, and thus the Folio reads. But critics, with the ostrich still in their thoughts, could not understand the allusion, and chose to read

> All plumed like estridges (ostriches) that wing the wind;
> Bated like eagles having lately bathed.

> This emendation labours under the disadvantage that it reduces to nonsense what is at all events intelligible. The only objection to what Shakespeare wrote is that the

feathers of a goshawk, bating and fluttering with the wind, do not afford so striking a simile as the plumes of an ostrich. But if this objection did not occur to Shakespeare we need not trouble ourselves about it. The Cambridge editors obelize the passage. But I have followed Dr Schmidt (*Shakespeare Lexicon*) in accepting the text of the Folio, which is clear enough when the meaning of the technical terms of falconry is understood.

This is how Dyce comments on the lines. First of all, he punctuates them like this:

> All furnish'd, all in arms;
> All plum'd like estridges that wing the wind;
> Bated like eagles having lately bath'd;

The emendation *wing* for *with* is called Dr Johnson's emendation, and was adopted by Rowe. Dyce accepts it, "not only", he says, "because it affords a clear and good meaning, but because it is far from improbable that *wing* might have been mistaken by a transcriber or compositor for *with*, in which word, in the handwriting of the poet's time, the head of the *h* is often found carried below the line". Then he has to account for *bated*. "*Bated*, as Malone observes, would seem to be used here for *bating* (fluttering), the passive for the active (the past for the present) participle. There is a double comparison: the prince and his followers are compared first to ostriches, and secondly to eagles. In what sense *the ostrich* may be said to *wing the wind*, we are beautifully told by Claudian, who, if he was a native of Alexandria, might not have had to trust entirely to his fancy for a picture, which indeed has quite the air of having been taken from the life:

> Vasta velut Libyae venantum vocibus ales
> cum premitur, calidas cursu transmittit arenas,
> *inque modum veli sinuatis flamine pennis*
> *pulverulenta volat.*
>
> > *In Eutrop.* II. 310–314."

Douce, in his *Illustrations of Shakespeare*, 1807, said Shakespeare wrote of the estridge or goshawk, not of the ostrich, when he made Enobarbus say of Antony:

> Now he'll outstare the lightning. To be furious
> Is to be frighted out of fear; and in that mood
> The dove will peck the estridge.

Dyce comments on this as follows:

> The absurdity of Douce's remarks on this passage is beyond belief: he labours to prove that by *estridges* we are not to understand "ostriches" but estridge *falcons*; and that too in the very face of lines quoted by Steevens from Drayton's *Polyolbion*:
>
>> Prince Edward all in gold, as he great Jove had been;
>> De Mountfords all in plumes, like estridges, were seen.

The Cambridge editors followed the Folio (except that they omitted the commas after *Estridges* and *Eagles* and *bath'd* that are in the First Folio), and affirmed that Dyce's quotation from Claudian was not to the purpose, for it "means that the bird spreads its wings like a sail bellying with the wind—a different thing from 'winging the wind'". Dyce goes on to say that the Cambridge editors in expounding the Latin lines forgot the important word *volat*, by which, says Dyce, "he means of course that the ostrich *when once her wings are filled with the wind*, FLIES *along the ground*, though she does not mount into the air". This passage of arms between the critics suggests a few things to the lay mind. We know that in Shakespeare's time terms of falconry were as well known and as commonly used by the great public as racing terms are at the present day. We know that the word "estridge" was sometimes used to mean a goshawk. Mr Madden says: "Those who, like Shakespeare, were careful to use terms of art aright, distinguished the 'falconer' who pursued his quarry with the long-winged hawk or falcon, from the 'astringer'.* The latter was so called from the goshawk or estridge (French *Austour* or *autour*; Latin *astur*), the representative of the race of short-winged hawks. We see in

* Cf. *All's Well that Ends Well*, Act v, Scene 3: "Enter a gentle astringer."

the passage quoted from *Antony and Cleopatra* that Shakespeare used the word estridge to mean a hawk; at least it is unlikely that he would have said that an angry dove would peck an ostrich."

Estridge is used, meaning goshawk, in other works contemporary with Shakespeare, or prior to him, for instance in the *Romance of Guy of Warwick**. The hoods of hawks were plumed when taken out for falconry. *Bating* or *bated* was a very common term meaning fluttering or beating the wings. Lastly, as far as we know, the word written by Shakespeare was *with* and not *wing*, and if we substitute *wing* we have to do violence to the grammar and the sense. Personally I believe Shakespeare meant a goshawk and not an ostrich, and I think that in the passage quoted by Dyce from Drayton he may quite well have meant to compare De Mountfords to hawks too, and not to ostriches; at least I not only think one just as likely as the other, I feel quite sure that Shakespeare meant a hawk. The alternative for the reader is this: Did Shakespeare write

> All plum'd like estridges that with the wind
> Bated like eagles, having lately bath'd,

and did the Folio print this right, and did he mean that the Prince of Wales and his companions were like goshawks with their plumed hoods ready to be flown, and beating their wings, like eagles lately bathed; or did he write

> All plum'd like estridges that wing the wind;
> Bated like eagles having lately bath'd;

and did the printers of the Folio make a mistake; and did Shakespeare mean that they were (A) plumed like ostriches that skim along the ground with wind in their wings, and (B) seen at the same time like eagles who, after bathing, fluttered, that is to say, beat their wings (using the passive for the active and the past for the present)? The second theory (B) seems a great deal more complicated, especially as Shakespeare constantly uses the technical terms of falconry for similes. Also, one would

---

* The Emperour sent for his fowlis thoo,
 Ostreyes and faukons, girfaukes also.

[213]

think it likely that Shakespeare would compare something to a falcon rather than to an ostrich.

Another point: If Dyce's supposition is true, the transcriber or compositor not only misread *with* for *wing*, but he inserted the comma after *Eagles* which exists in the Folio, and suppressed semi-colons at the end of each of the first three lines which do not exist in the Folio.

Anyone who is interested in the subject will find D. H. Madden's *Diary of Master William Silence* the most enchanting reading.

A part le comédien, le prince et l'évêque, il est un homme
à la fois prince et comédien, un homme revêtu d'un
magnifique sacerdoce, le poète, qui semble ne rien faire
et qui néanmoins règne sur l'humanité, quand il a su la
peindre.

Balzac, *Illusions Perdues*.

Penser, rêver, concevoir de belles œuvres, est une occupation délicieuse, c'est fumer des cigares enchantés.

Id. La Cousine Bette.

Oui, elle est belle, mais moi je me sens: je suis pire.

Id. ib.

I suppose if there were a plebiscite held in France as to who
was the greatest French novelist, Balzac would assuredly come
out top of the list. He had certain affinities with Dickens which
are not only due to his belonging to the same epoch. His eyes,
like those of Dickens, seem to me more powerful and penetrating
than those of ordinary mortals. They were more like magnifying
glasses than eyes. That is why both in Dickens and in Balzac
you sometimes get the effect of a certain distortion. They saw
what was there; but they saw more, and more deeply, than other
people. In addition to this, Balzac has a kind of obsessive power.
He holds you with his glittering eye, like the Ancient Mariner;
and once you take a plunge into a book of his you are obsessed
by it as by a dream, in spite of its great reality of detail. Tolstoi's
realism is different. His people are so real and yet so
ordinary that you seem to distinguish the accents of their
different voices. When I was young, people used to say that
Balzac wrote badly, and that you must admire him in spite of
his writing. Now they say he writes well. That is a question of
argument.

H

There can be no question about Chateaubriand, who comes next in my luggage. There is no doubt that he wrote well. Here are a few sentences:

Chaque pommier, avec ses fleurs carminées, ressemble à un gros bouquet de fiancée de village.

La charrue et la barque, à un jet de pierre l'une de l'autre, sillonnent la terre et l'eau.

La mort est belle, elle est notre amie: néanmoins nous ne la reconnaissons pas, parce qu'elle se présente à nous masquée et que son masque nous épouvante.

Le vent du soir qui brisait les réseaux tendus par l'insecte sur la pointe des herbes, l'alouette de bruyère qui se posait sur un caillou, me rappelaient à la réalité.

Elle a passé comme une ombre charmante dans ma vie.

Les chouettes, voletant d'une tour à l'autre, passant et repassant entre la lune et moi, dessinaient sur mes rideaux l'ombre mobile de leurs ailes.

Des sables de diverses couleurs, des bancs variés de coquillages, des varechs, des franges d'une écume argentée, dessinent la lisière blonde ou verte des blés.

Les ruines baignées dans une rosée de lumière dorée, transparente, volage, que réfléchissaient les mers, que répandaient comme un parfum les zéphyres de Salamine et de Délos.

Les animaux de la création veillaient; la terre, en adoration, semblait encenser le ciel, et l'ombre exhalée de son sein retombait sur elle en rosée comme la prière redescend sur celui qui prie.

Le vieux matelot ressemble au vieux laboureur. Leurs moissons sont différentes, il est vrai: le matelot a mené une vie errante, le laboureur n'a jamais quitté son champ; mais ils connaissent également les étoiles et prédisent l'avenir en creusant leurs sillons.

Elle me dégoûtait de tout, car j'en faisais un objet perpétuel de comparaison à son avantage.

Les années qui avaient passé sur sa tête ne lui avaient laissé que leur printemps.

Sa beauté portait l'empreinte de la main divine qui l'avait pétrie.

Douce lueur du passé, rose pâle du crépuscule qui borde la nuit, quand le soleil depuis longtemps est couché.

L'on ne vit que par le style. En vain on se révolte contre cette vérité. L'ouvrage le mieux composé, orné de portraits d'une bonne ressemblance, rempli de mille autres perfections, est mort-né si le style manque. Le style, et il y en a de mille sortes, ne s'apprend pas; c'est le don du ciel, c'est le talent.

Les poètes sont des oiseaux: tout bruit les fait chanter.

La cime dorée des forêts.

These passages and sentences are not only beautifully phrased, they are not only exquisite examples of chosen language, but they are illumined by vision; they are shot with inspiration; they reflect the soul of a poet. And that is the whole point of Chateaubriand—he did not write prose poetry, but he wrote good prose, and, as he wrote it, never ceased to think like a poet. This does not mean that he does not every now and then say shrewd and notable things; for instance, he said that the French go instinctively for power; they do not care for liberty; equality is their idol. But as a rule, the more poetical the subject, the higher the flights of his style. For instance, this sentence about Rome, which reminds one of Byron:

Législatrice du monde, Rome, assise sur la pierre de son sépulcre, avec sa robe de siècles, projette le dessin irrégulier de sa grande figure dans la solitude lactée.

He also says:

La mort semble née à Rome.

It is Chateaubriand who recorded that Napoleon said he

[217]

refused to serve with a man who thought he was the first general in the Empire, and that he thought one bad general was better than two good ones. It was Chateaubriand who said that Talleyrand claimed to be a prophet and had always been wrong ("Il se crut prophète en se trompant sur tout").

He bewailed the infidelity of his time: "Le temps du désert est revenu; le christianisme recommencera dans la stérilité de la Thébaïde, au milieu d'une idolatrie redoutable, l'idolatrie de l'homme envers soi."

Nobody ever wrote more beautiful prose than Chateaubriand, and, as I have already said, he succeeded in being poetical without writing "prose poetry". I am often asked who is considered to be the best prose writer in Russian, and my answer is: It depends on your standards and your taste in such matters; that is to say, if your ideal of prose is complete simplicity, absence of rhetoric, lucidity and ease, all the qualities which distinguish the prose of Voltaire, for instance, then there is no doubt that the first of Russian prose writers is the man who is the first of Russian poets, namely, Pushkin. Next to him would come Tolstoi, and then, some way after, Turgenev and Dostoievski. That is, if your ideal is that prose should be like a pianoforte without a pedal, as André Gide said of the French language. The prose of Turgenev is more like Chateaubriand's than Flaubert's; it is imaginative, musical, pictorial and fraught with beauty, and yet easy. The prose of Tolstoi is simple and natural, without rhetoric or emphasis, and extraordinarily vivid. The prose of Dostoievski used to be thought bad, as he evidently bothered little about style, but it was the only instrument fit and appropriate for his great imaginings and the great convulsions and tempests and cataclysms of soul that he portrayed. It is like Emily Brontë's prose. It was found, when certain chapters of *The Brothers Karamazov* were performed at the Art Theatre in Moscow, that not a word of the dialogue could be changed, and it got across the footlights as it was written.

Talking of style, and natural style, Pascal says (there will be more Pascal later):

Quand on voit le style naturel, on est tout étonné et ravi;

car on s'attendait de voir un auteur, et on trouve un homme.

Here is another remark of Pascal:

> De ce que la religion chrétienne n'est pas unique, ce n'est pas une raison de croire qu'elle n'est pas la véritable. Au contraire, c'est ce qui fait voir qu'elle l'est.

Now come some fragments of Corneille. First of all, a very famous one, quoted in grammars as an example of oxymoron:

> Cette obscure clarté qui tombe des étoiles
> Enfin avec le flux nous fait voir trente voiles.

Here are some more lines:

> Ne désespère pas une âme qui t'adore.

> Dieu même a craint la mort.

Madame de Sévigné could not understand anybody admiring Racine more than Corneille; and it is certainly true that Corneille touches heights of sublimity to which no other French poet ever attained, and he often does it in a few words, sometimes in one word. For instance, in the famous piece of dialogue in his play on Medea:

> Votre pays vous hait, votre époux est sans foi,
> Dans un si grand revers que vous reste-t-il?
> *Médée.*   Moi,

I once heard Mr Desmond MacCarthy say about a certain person:

> He never read a book from a sense of duty in his life, and yet he arrives at the same conclusions which people who pore over books, obsessed by a severe sense of duty, with difficulty reach; as for instance, that Corneille is perhaps the greatest of French poets.

Among the Corneille comes a line of Homer from the *Odyssey*:

> αὐτὰρ ἐμοὶ καὶ πένθος ἀμέτρητον πόρε δαίμων.

But to me the deity brought measureless sorrow.

Now I come to a fragment from the correspondence of Flaubert.

> Chaque rêve finit par trouver sa forme; il y a des ondes pour toutes les soifs, de l'amour pour tous les cœurs.

Three fragments of Milton:

                    till we end
In dust, our final rest and native home.

Paradise Lost.

                    And moving light
More orient in yon western cloud, that draws
O'er the blue firmament a radiant white,
And slow descends, with something heavenly fraught.

Id.

So much I feel my genial spirits droop,
My hopes all flat: Nature within me seems
In all her functions weary of herself;
My race of glory run, and race of shame,
And I shall shortly be with them that rest.

Samson Agonistes.

And with Milton there are several fragments from Pascal:

> Jésus Christ est un Dieu dont on s'approche sans orgueil, et sous lequel on s'abaisse sans désespoir.

> L'homme n'est qu'un roseau le plus faible de la nature: mais c'est un roseau pensant.

> Car enfin, qu'est-ce que l'homme dans la nature? Un néant à l'égard de l'infini, un tout à l'égard du néant, un milieu entre rien et tout.

H*

Perhaps the founder of modern French prose, with its ideals of harmony and proportion, of lucidity and order, and lack of emphasis and exaggeration, was La Bruyère. Here are one or two of his sentences:

Un beau visage est le plus beau de tous les spectacles, et l'harmonie la plus douce est le son de la voix de celle que l'on aime.

La vie est courte et ennuyeuse; elle se passe toute à désirer.

Les enfants n'ont ni passé, ni avenir; et, ce qui nous n'arrive guère, ils jouissent du présent.

Être avec les gens qu'on aime, cela suffit: rêver, leur parler, ne leur parler point, penser à eux, penser à des choses plus indifférentes, mais auprès d'eux, tout est égal.

Il faut juger des femmes depuis la chaussure jusqu'à la coiffure exclusivement, à peu près comme on mesure le poisson entre queue et tête.

Si les femmes étaient telles naturellement qu'elles le deviennent par artifice, qu'elles perdissent en un moment toute la fraîcheur de leur teint, qu'elles eussent le visage aussi allumé et aussi plombé qu'elles se le font par le rouge et par la peinture dont elles se fardent, elles seraient inconsolables.

Oh, it's sure a crime the way we torture some o' the white souls 'at drift to this Sorrowful Star, as I once heard a feller call it.

Those people who know precisely the right time to disobey orders are a big help to humanity, but they're mighty scarce.

R. A. Wason.

Mais ce qu'une honnête et spirituelle femme comme elle entendait par bien marier sa fille, on aurait peine à le concevoir, si l'on ne voyait tous les jours que l'expérience personelle la plus douloureuse, l'amour maternel le plus vrai, l'esprit le plus délicat et même la piété la plus haute ne suffisent pas à enseigner aux mères la différence d'un beau mariage et d'un bon mariage.

Octave Feuillet.

He seemed to march towards crime with the monstrous innocence of Oedipus.

G. K. Chesterton.

Prayer, like generalship, must sometimes be daring. To ask a king for a trifle is to insult him. The thief daringly asked Jesus to give him the Kingdom of Heaven—to give it in a moment—and to give it after a life of sin. And it was given to him, even as he prayed.

Father Vincent McNabb.

Prayer moves an arm that is almighty; and that arm moves the world.

Id.

All desire is a prophecy.

Id.

Many prayers seem to be unanswered because God has answered them before we prayed.

Id.

Nous arrivons tout nouveaux aux divers âges de la vie.
La Rochefoucauld.

It is impossible to be just to the Catholic Church. The moment men cease to pull against it, they feel a tug towards it.

G. K. Chesterton.

La religion catholique, c'est tout à fait autre chose, mon amie, croyez-moi; c'est beaucoup, beaucoup plus que jamais, jusqu'ici, il ne vous a été donné d'entrevoir.

This sentence comes from a modern French novel; but I have forgotten the name of the author, and cannot trace it. Mallock wrote some interesting things on this theme; for instance:

> In this country the popular conception of Rome has been so distorted by our familiarity with Protestantism, that the true conception of her is something quite strange to us. Our divines have exhibited her to us as though she were a lapsed Protestant sect, and they have attacked her for being false to doctrines that were never really hers.
>
> They have failed to see that the first and essential difference which separates her from them lies primarily, not in any special dogma, but in the authority on which all her dogma rests. Protestants, basing their religion on the Bible solely, have conceived that Catholics of course profess to do so likewise; and have covered them with invective for being traitors to their supposed profession.
>
> But the Church's primary doctrine is her own perpetual infallibility. She is inspired, she declares, by the same spirit that inspired the Bible; and her voice is, equally with the Bible, the voice of God.
>
> Looked at in this way, Rome to the Protestants must have seemed naturally to be a mass of superstitions and dishonesties; and it is this view of her that, strangely enough, our modern advanced thinkers have accepted without question. Though they have trusted the Protestants in nothing else, they have trusted them here. They have taken the Protestant's word for it, that Protestantism is more reasonable than Romanism; and they think, therefore, that if they have destroyed the former, *à fortiori* they have destroyed the latter.

If we would obtain a true view of the general character of the Catholic Church, we must begin by making a clean sweep of all the views that, as outsiders, we have been taught to entertain about her.

We must in the first place learn to conceive of her as a living, spiritual body, as infallible and as authoritative now as she ever was, with her eyes undimmed and her strength not abated, continuing to grow still as she has continued to grow hitherto: and the growth of the new dogmas that she may from time to time enunciate, we must learn to see, are, from her standpoint, signs of life and not signs of corruption.

And further, when we come to look into her more closely, we must separate carefully the diverse elements we find in her—her discipline, her pious opinions, her theology, and her religion.

Is Life Worth Living?

Later on he says that the outside world only reaches Catholic doctrine through explanation,

...and the explanation or the account of anything is always far more intricate than the apprehension of the thing itself. Not only does the intricacy of Catholicism described blind them to the simplicity of Catholicism experienced, but they confuse with the points of faith not only the scientific accounts of them which theologians give, but the mere rules of discipline and pious opinions.

Is Life Worth Living?

Talking of the Catholic Church, he says:

She cannot be outside progress because she herself is everywhere. What she rejects in the spirit of modern secularism is not its truths, but its false and delirious expression of them.

A Romance of the Nineteenth Century.

Into the great Temple of Truth, the Church of God, there are two gates—the gate of wisdom and the gate of beauty. I am inclined to think that the narrow gate is the gate of wisdom, and the wide gate, through which millions pass, is the gate of beauty. The Catholic Church has these portals ever open. She welcomes from time to time the few philosophers and thinkers who crucify themselves by thought, but she welcomes unceasingly the countless numbers who come for her colour, for her song, for her smile—as they go afield for the warmth and light of the spring sun. I believe the way of beauty is the wiser as well as the wider way. It is God's own most perfect thoroughfare—God's way to Himself.

Father Vincent McNabb.

My experience convinced me that the actor must imagine first and observe afterwards. It is no good observing life and bringing the result to the stage without selection, without a definite idea. The idea must come first, the realism afterwards.

Ellen Terry.

This is true about other arts besides that of the stage. The idea must come first. It is the seed of all artistic production. The realism and the observation come of their own accord when they are wanted. Marcel Proust writes on this subject, and says that the man of letters envies the painter and would like to make sketches and take notes, and he goes on to say:

Il est perdu s'il le fait. Mais quand il écrit, il n'est pas un geste de ses personnages, un tic, un accent, qui n'ait été apporté à son inspiration par sa mémoire, il n'est pas un nom de personnage inventé sous lequel il ne puisse mettre soixante noms de personnages vus, dont l'un a posé pour la grimace, l'autre pour le monocle, tel pour la colère, tel pour le mouvement avantageux du bras, etc. Et alors l'écrivain se rend compte que si son rêve d'être un peintre n'était pas réalisable d'une manière consciente et volontaire il se trouve pourtant avoir été réalisé et que l'écrivain lui aussi a fait son carnet de croquis sans le savoir....

Le temps retrouvé.

His idea is that all imaginative work, all fiction, is the fruit of memory, that the memory must be unconscious, it cannot be harnessed or organized into notebooks. If you keep notes, by the time you want to use them you have forgotten what they are about. Memory is the greatest of artists, and effaces from your mind what is unnecessary. What is necessary and what is wanted comes mysteriously at the beck and call of the artist. I remember when I was writing a novel called *Cat's Cradle* I wanted a name for an Italian prince who marries the heroine. As I was wondering what name I could invent or copy, there came into my head a song sung by Corney Grain in an entertainment which used to be given on Saturday afternoons called

[234]

the "German Reeds". At the end of it Corney Grain sat at the pianoforte and gave a musical sketch. For one of his sketches he invented a parody of a Neapolitan song, which was made up of the names of Italian railway stations. He said he had found one gorgeous name, which was that of a small station in Sicily, and which was *Roccapalumba*. I was twelve years old when I heard Corney Grain sing this song, and it was thirty-six years later that the name of this railway station, which up till then had remained dormant, came at the call and bidding of invention. It was just what I wanted.

Les femmes ne connaissent pas toute leur coquéterie.

La Rochefoucauld.

Ma surprise n'est pas que l'homme ait besoin d'une religion; ce qui m'étonne, c'est qu'il se croie jamais assez fort, assez à l'abri du malheur pour oser en rejeter une.

Benjamin Constant.

Il n'a pas l'intelligence assez large pour concevoir que l'intérêt n'est pas seul à mener le monde, qu'il se mêle souvent et qu'il cède parfois à des passions plus fortes, voire à des passions nobles.

Maurice Barrès

The grand object of travelling is to see the shores of the Mediterranean.

Dr Johnson.

Violent pain of mind, like violent pain of body, must be severely felt.

Id.

A man who is good enough to go to heaven is good enough to be a clergyman.

Id.

Any society has a right to preserve public peace and order, and therefore has a good right to prohibit the propagation of opinions which have a dangerous tendency. To say the magistrate has this right is using an inadequate word: it is the society for which the magistrate is agent.

Id.

(Of common sports) he (Dr Johnson) once pleasantly remarked to me, "How wonderfully well he continued to be idle without them."

Boswell.

Sir, your levellers wish to level down as far as themselves, but they cannot bear levelling up to themselves.

Dr Johnson.

Small crocuses defy the rage of days,
With golden eye they spy upon the spring.

Loyd Haberly.

Ne les détournez pas, ces yeux qui me déchirent,
Ces yeux tendres, ces yeux perçants, mais amoureux,
Qui semblent partager le trouble qu'ils m'inspirent.
Hélas! plus ils sont dangereux,
Plus je me plais à m'attacher sur eux!
Par quel ordre du ciel que je ne puis comprendre,
Vous dis-je plus que je ne dois?
Moi de qui la pudeur devrait du moins attendre
Que l'amour m'expliquât le trouble où je vous vois.
Vous soupirez, seigneur, ainsi que je soupire;
Vos sens, comme les miens, paraissent interdits,
C'est à moi de m'en taire,—à vous de me le dire,
Et cependant c'est moi qui vous le dis.

Molière, Psyché.

The following poem by Lermontov is one of the most characteristic, not only of that poet's work, but of all Russian poetry: it is written in the language of ordinary everyday conversation; it is written in the vernacular, without indulging in slang, and the result is poignant poetry:

Завѣщаніе

Наединѣ съ тобою, братъ,
Хотѣлъ бы я побыть:
На свѣтѣ мало, говорятъ,
Мнѣ остается жить!
Поѣдешь скоро ты домой:
Смотри жъ.... Да что! моей судьбой
Сказать по правдѣ, очень
Никто не озабоченъ.

А если спроситъ кто-нибудь...
Ну, кто бы ни спросилъ, —
Скажи имъ, что на вылетъ въ грудь
Я пулей раненъ былъ;
Что умеръ, честно за царя,
Что плохи наши лѣкаря,
И что родному краю
Поклонъ я посылаю.

Отца и мать мою едва ль
Застанешь ты въ живыхъ...
Признаться, право, было бъ жаль
Мнѣ опечалить ихъ;
Но если кто изъ нихъ и живъ,
Скажи, что я писать лѣнивъ,
Что полкъ въ походъ послали,
И чтобъ меня не ждали.

Сосѣдка есть у нихъ одна...
Какъ вспомнишь, какъ давно
Разстались.... Обо мнѣ она
Не спроситъ.... Все равно,
Ты разскажи всю правду ей,
Пустого сердца не жалѣй—
Пускай она поплачетъ...
Ей ничего не значитъ!...

[242]

Here is my attempt at a translation:

Testament

I want to be alone with you,
  A moment quite alone.
The minutes left to me are few,
  They say I'll soon be gone.
And you are going home on leave,
Then say...but why? I do believe
There's not a soul, who'll greatly care
To hear about me over there.

And yet if someone questions you,
  Whoever it may be,—
Tell them a bullet hit me through
  The chest,—and did for me.
And say I died, and for the Tsar,
And say what fools the doctors are:—
And that I shook you by the hand,
And spoke about my native land.

My father and my mother, both,
  By now are surely dead—
To tell the truth, I would be loth
  To send them tears to shed.
If one of them is living, say
I'm bad at writing home, and they
Have told the regiment to pack,—
And that I shan't be coming back.

We had a neighbour, as you know,
  And you remember I
And she....How very long ago
  It is we said good-bye!
She won't ask after me, nor care,
But tell her ev'rything, don't spare
Her empty heart; and let her cry;—
To her it doesn't signify.

I have worked at this translation for years. This is the best I can
do; but apart from being inadequate, it is not quite right.

I find Lermontov still more difficult to translate than Pushkin.
Here is a poem of Pushkin's:

Воспоминаніе

Когда для смертнаго умолкнетъ шумный день
И на нѣмыя стогны града
Полупрозрачная наляжетъ ночи тѣнь
И сонъ, дневныхъ трудовъ награда,
Въ то время для меня влачатся въ тишинѣ
Часы томительнаго бдѣнья:
Въ бездѣйствіи ночномъ живѣй горятъ во мнѣ
Змѣи сердечной угрызенья;
Мечты кипятъ; въ умѣ, подавленномъ тоской
Тѣснится тяжкихъ думъ избытокъ;
Воспоминаніе безмолвно предо мной
Свой длинный развиваетъ свитокъ:
И съ отвращеніемъ читая жизнь мою,
Я трепещу и проклинаю,
И горько жалуюсь, и горько слезы лью,
Но строкъ печальныхъ не смываю.

Remembrance

When the loud day for men who sow and reap
Grows still, and on the silence of the town
The unsubstantial veils of night and sleep,
The meed of the day's labour, settle down,
Then for me in the stillness of the night
The wasting, watchful hours drag on their course,
And in the idle darkness comes the bite
Of all the burning serpents of remorse;
Dreams seethe; and fretful infelicities
Are swarming in my over-burdened soul,
And Memory before my wakeful eyes
With noiseless hand unwinds her lengthy scroll.
Then, as with loathing I peruse the years,
I tremble, and I curse my natal day,
Wail bitterly, and bitterly shed tears,
But cannot wash the woeful script away.

[244]

Pushkin's most famous poem is *The Prophet*:

Пророкъ

Духовной жаждою томимъ,
Въ пустынѣ мрачной я влачился,
И шестикрылый серафимъ
На перепутьѣ мнѣ явился;
Перстами, легкими какъ сонъ,
Моихъ зѣницъ коснулся онъ:
Отверзлись вѣщія зѣницы,
Какъ у испуганной орлицы.
Моихъ ушей коснулся онъ,
И ихъ наполнилъ шумъ и звонъ:
И внялъ я неба содроганье,
И горній ангеловъ полетъ,
И гадъ морскихъ подводный ходъ,
И дольней лозы прозябанье.
И онъ къ устамъ моимъ приникъ,
И вырвалъ грѣшный мой языкъ,
И празднословный, и лукавый,
И жало мудрыя змѣи
Въ уста замершія мои
Вложилъ десницею кровавой.
И онъ мнѣ грудь разсѣкъ мечомъ,
И сердце трепетное вынулъ,
И угль, пылающій огнемъ,
Во грудь отверстую водвинулъ.
Какъ трупъ въ пустынѣ я лежалъ,
И Бога гласъ ко мнѣ воззвалъ:
„Возстань, пророкъ, и виждь, и внемли,
Исполнись волею Моей,
И обходя моря и земли,
Глаголомъ жги сердца людей!"

Here is my attempt at a translation, which has found favour
with some Russian readers:

[245]

With fainting soul athirst for Grace,
I wandered in a desert place,
And at the crossing of the ways
I saw the sixfold Seraph blaze;
He touched mine eyes with fingers light
As sleep that cometh in the night:
And like a frighted eagle's eyes,
They opened wide with prophecies.
He touched mine ears, and they were drowned
With tumult and a roaring sound:
I heard convulsion in the sky,
And flights of angel hosts on high,
And beasts that move beneath the sea,
And the sap creeping in the tree.
And bending to my mouth he wrung
From out of it my sinful tongue,
And all its lies and idle rust,
And 'twixt my lips a-perishing
A subtle serpent's forkèd sting
With right hand wet with blood he thrust.
And with his sword my breast he cleft,
My quaking heart thereout he reft,
And in the yawning of my breast
A coal of living fire he pressed.
Then in the desert I lay dead,
And God called unto me and said:
"Arise, and let My voice be heard,
Charged with My Will go forth and span
The land and sea, and let My Word
Lay waste with fire the heart of man."

BOSWELL: "The idolatry of the Mass?" JOHNSON: "Sir, there is no idolatry in the Mass. They believe God to be there, and they adore him." BOSWELL: "The worship of Saints?" JOHNSON: "Sir, they do not worship saints; they invoke them; they only ask their prayers."

Boswell.

The anguish of life is, that a good man finds he is doing things with mixed motives. This clear-sightedness is, in reality, humility, if humility be the seeing of things in proportion, including yourself.

Father C. C. Martindale, S.J.

L'amour est l'art de conquérir, de posséder, de retenir
une âme si riche qu'elle nous soulève, et si pauvre
qu'elle ait de nous le besoin que nous avons d'elle.

Paul Géraldy.

Au fond, toute âme humaine est cela…: une fragile lumière en marche vers quelque abri divin, qu'elle imagine, cherche et ne voit pas.

André Maurois.

The water of conviction is changed into the wine of faith.
Father Ronald Knox.

Cada uno es artifice de sa ventura.

Don Quixote.

Everyone is the artificer of his own misfortune.

This reminds me of a sentence of John Oliver Hobbes, noted in 1892:

> Men heap together the mistakes of their lives, and create a monster which they call Destiny. Some take a mournful pleasure in contemplating the ugliness of the idol: these are called Stoics. Others build it a temple like Solomon's, and worship the temple. These are called Epicureans.
>
> *The Sinner's Comedy.*

The younger a man is, the less he believes in goodness, though he is more credulous of evil.

Tolstoi

In 1799 General Tamac received a proposal from Napoleon, who wished to enter the Russian service, but they were unable to agree, as Napoleon demanded the rank of Major.

Id.

(It is also said that when Napoleon was a schoolboy his father hesitated between sending him into the French Army or the British Navy.)

Avoid contradicting in general, especially people you love!

Id.

Galileo keeps on harping on how things happen, when his adversaries had a complete theory as to why things happened.

Whitehead.

A child once asked what was a cow, and it was explained to him that a cow was an animal with four feet, horns and other attributes. The child then asked: "*Why* is a cow?" That was more difficult to answer.

They all insisted, "It is art for art's sake that is being discussed", that every picture is as impersonal as a pattern. They ought to have insisted that every pattern is as personal as a picture. Whether or no we see faces in the carpet, we ought to see a mind in the carpet; and in fact, there is a mind in every scheme of ornament. There is as emphatically a morality expressed in Babylonian architecture or baroque architecture as if it were plastered all over with Biblical texts.

Literature is but language; it is only a rare and amazing miracle by which a man really says what he means.

G. K. Chesterton.

Elle ne parlait que par nuances; jamais elle n'a dit un
bon mot: c'était quelque chose de trop exprimé. Les
bons mots se retiennent; elle ne voulait que plaire et
perdre ce qu'elle disait.

Talleyrand on his Mother, from *Talleyrand* by Jacques Sindral.

Talleyrand's mother as here described must have possessed
the quintessence and the rarest form of true wit; that wit which
is forgotten as soon as it is born, because it is so exquisitely
appropriate to its context, to the time and place at which it is
said, and to all the circumstances which give it birth, that it
cannot be torn from them; and it is here that it differs from
epigram. Epigram is remembered for a time, but if it is merely
brilliant without being profound, it soon has an appearance of
tarnished tinsel. Boswell once said: "When I complained of
having dined at a splendid table without hearing one sentence
of conversation worthy to be remembered, he (Dr Johnson) said,
'There is seldom any such conversation.'" Whenever Oscar
Wilde's comedies are revived in modern times, the epigrams in
them have mostly an air of faded tinsel, but the wit that is
inherent in the situations, and which is in fact comedy in action,
survives.

The mention of Johnson leads me to several scraps noted at different times:

Approve it only;—'tis too late to praise—

The better a man is, the more afraid he should be of death, having a clearer view of infinite purity.

Don't you know it is very uncivil to *pit* two people against one another?

Goldsmith was a man who, whatever he wrote, did it better than any other man could do.

People seldom read a book which is given them, and few are given. The way to spread a work is to sell it at a low price.

There is no profession to which a man gives a very great proportion of his time.

No man is obliged to do as much as he can. A man is to have a part of his life to himself.

A boy being flogged at school is not so severe as a man having the hiss of the world against him.

No man fond of letters leaves London without regret.

Das Jahr klingt ab. Der Wind geht über die Stoppeln und findet nichts mehr zu bewegen; nur die rothen Beeren jener schlanken Bäume scheinen uns noch an etwas Munteres erinnern zu wollen, so wie uns der Taktschlag des Dreschers, daß in der abgesichelten Aehre so viel Nährendes und Lebendiges verborgen liegt.

The year is drawing to a close. The wind passes over the stubble and finds nothing more to move; only the red berries of those slender trees seem to wish to remind us of something bright, just as the beat of the thresher sets us thinking of so much nourishment and life lying concealed in the reaped ears of corn.

This passage comes from Goethe's *Elective Affinities*, a novel which is seldom read by people under fifty, and seldom by those over fifty; but when it is read it is enjoyed.

In this book one of the characters talks of marriage as follows:

Marriage is the beginning and the end of all culture, it civilizes the savage and gives the most cultured the best opportunity of displaying their delicacy. It must be indissoluble, for it brings so much happiness that any exceptional unhappinesses it may bring with it are, when weighed in the scales against the happiness, of no account. There can never be any adequate reason for separation. The scale of joy and sorrow in mortal affairs is so high that the sum which two married people owe one another is incalculable. It is an infinite debt, which can only be discharged throughout eternity.

In another part of the same book he says that great defects are inseparable from human existence:

If our old friends could shed certain of their peculiarities we should not like them.

Que voulez-vous? La perfection absolue fait toujours plaisir.

Jules Lemaître.

Dieu condamne certains hommes de génie à errer dans la tempête et à créer dans la douleur. Je t'ai assez étudié dans tes ombres et dans ta lumière, dans ta grandeur et dans ta faiblesse, pour savoir que tu es la victime d'une destinée, et que tu ne dois pas être pesé dans la même balance que la plupart des autres hommes. Ta souffrance et ton doute, ce que tu appelles ton châtiment, c'est peut-être la condition de ta gloire. Apprends donc à le subir. Tu as aspiré de toutes tes forces à l'idéal du bonheur, et tu ne l'as saisi que dans tes rêves. Eh bien, tes rêves, mon enfant, c'est ta réalité à toi, c'est ton talent, c'est ta vie; n'est-tu pas artiste?

Sois tranquille, va, Dieu te pardonnera de n'avoir pu aimer. Il t'avait condamné à cette insatiable aspiration pour que ta jeunesse ne fût pas absorbée par une femme. Les femmes de l'avenir, celles qui contempleront ton œuvre, de siècle en siècle, voilà tes sœurs et tes amantes.

George Sand.

This is what the heroine says to the hero in George Sand's novel *Elle et Lui*, which is as much the love story of herself and Alfred de Musset as his book, *La Confession d'un Enfant du Siècle*. In the passage just quoted it is she herself speaking to Musset himself, and diagnosing his case with acute sympathy. They each of them made copy out of their love story, and the most beautiful literary fruit of it was a speech in Musset's charming comedy, *On ne badine pas avec l'Amour*, which originally occurred in a letter from Musset to George Sand:

Adieu, Camille, retourne à ton couvent, et lorsqu'on te fera de ces récits hideux qui t'ont empoisonnée, réponds ce que je vais te dire: Tous les hommes sont menteurs, inconstants, faux, bavards, hypocrites, orgueilleux; ou lâches, méprisables et sensuels; toutes les femmes sont perfides, artificieuses, vaniteuses, curieuses et dépravées; le monde n'est qu'un égout sans fond; mais il y a au monde une chose sainte et sublime, c'est l'union de deux de ces êtres si imparfaits. On est souvent trompé en amour, souvent blessé et souvent malheureux; mais on aime, et quand on est sur le bord de sa tombe, on se retourne pour regarder en arrière, et on se dit: J'ai souffert souvent, je me suis trompé quelquefois, mais j'ai aimé. C'est moi qui ai vécu, et non pas un être factice créé par mon orgueil et mon ennui.

ces doux chants de la mort
Pareils aux chants plaintifs que murmure une femme
A l'enfant qui s'endort.

Lamartine.

My Anna Karenina gives me a feeling of nausea; she worries me like a puppy with an execrable disposition. But never tell me about her failings, or if you must, tell me with great consideration, for in spite of all I have adopted her.

Tolstoi, *Correspondence.*

There was little or no morning bank. A brightening came in the east; then a wash of some ineffable, faint nameless hue between crimson and silver; and then coals of fire. These glimmered a while on the sea-line, and seemed to brighten and darken and spread out, and still the night and stars reigned undisturbed; it was as though a spark should catch and glow and creep along the foot of some heavy and almost incombustible wall-hanging; and the room itself be scarce menaced. Yet a little after, and the whole east glowed with gold and scarlet, and the hollow of heaven was filled with daylight.

Stevenson, *The Ebb-Tide.*

It is interesting to compare this passage, which Stevenson wrote at the end of his life at Samoa, with another description of the dawn, from *Prince Otto,* which he wrote at the beginning of his career:

Soon she struggled to a certain hill-top, and saw far before her the silent inflooding of the day. Out of the east it welled and whitened; the darkness trembled into light; and the stars were extinguished like the street lamps of a human city. The whiteness brightened into silver, the silver warmed into gold, the gold kindled into pure and living fire; and the face of the east was barred with elemental scarlet. The day drew its first long breath, steady and chill; and for leagues around the woods sighed and shivered.

His opinion of the world affected her like a creature threatened with the deprivation of air.

Women

They are society's hard-drilled soldiery.

There is no freedom for the weak.

George Meredith.

Some future generation will have great fun in rebunking and rediscovering George Meredith. In France it is happening now: that is to say, he is being discovered for the first time. It has taken seventy years for his reputation to cross the Channel, and this discovery has come about just at a time of his total if temporary eclipse in England.

His *Modern Love* came out in 1862. His novels were neglected by his contemporaries until he was discovered by the young towards the end of the 'eighties and in the 'nineties. The young liked his works, and he presently became a shibboleth among the intellectuals. This lasted till 1914; then came first disparagement, and then neglect. His *Modern Love* has not been touched by Time. It is as "modern" now as it was when it was published. Nor can it be said that any of his novels are dated, for they have no date. The people in them, so far from belonging to any particular time or place, seem to belong to a different planet. They obey their own laws, and are true to them. What people find intolerable in his books now is the style, and that is just what his contemporaries found intolerable in them long ago. Yet you could not alter the style nor wish it away. It is as much a part of Meredith and as necessary to his qualities as Browning's uncouth rhythms were necessary to the power of his verse. One must just accept it. That is to say, one must accept being most of the time like a man walking through a forest in a fog, through prickles and brambles; sometimes the fog lifts, and you have a vision of such a dazzling purity of sky and stars that it is worth the discomfort of the journey.

Nay, rather every tedious stride I make
Will but remember me what deal of world
I wander from the jewels that I love.
Must I not serve a long apprenticehood
To foreign passages; and in the end,
Having my freedom, boast of nothing else
But that I was a journeyman to grief?

Shakespeare, *Richard II.*

On a tort de parler des consolations de la religion, dit
EnSénat—
     On doit dire: les terribles vérités chrétiennes.

Jacques Chardonne.

Yes; but people do not like being reminded of these terrible
truths; even when they are mentioned in the pulpit you will
notice the congregation receive a shock, and sometimes look
"shocked".

Il faut avoir le courage d'abandonner les enfants; leur
sagesse n'est pas la nôtre.

Id.

It is not in the storm nor in the strife
We feel benumb'd and wish to be no more,
But in the after-silence on the shore,
When all is lost except a little life.

Byron.

I once showed these lines, which are from the *Lines on hearing that Lady Byron was ill*, to a Frenchman, and he said: "On reconnaît la griffe du lion."

Byron has a quality in common with Shakespeare and Pope. He cannot really be parodied (though hundreds have attempted the task, from his own time to ours) because of the essential spring, the strength and gusto that is in him. This is seen in some of his most trivial poems; for instance, these lines on the bust of Helen by Canova could only have been written by Byron, and never by an imitator or a parodist of Byron.

In this beloved marble view,
    Above the works and thoughts of man,
What Nature *could*, but *would not*, do,
    And Beauty and Canova *can*!
Beyond imagination's power,
    Beyond the Bard's defeated art,
With immortality her dower,
    Behold the *Helen* of the *heart*!

Ce tiraillement perpétuel de deux hommes en lui: l'un
qui lui dit, quand tous ses effets sont prêts pour aller en
soirée: "Couche-toi, qu'est-ce que tu irais faire là?" et
l'autre qui lui dit, quand il est couché: "Tu aurais dû y
aller, tu te serais amusé."

Edmond de Goncourt.

On ne saura jamais combien les marchands de la pensée
et de l'écriture des autres sont bêtes.

Id.

Ce n'est pas la quantité de temps, ainsi qu'on le croit
généralement, qui fait la supériorité d'un livre, c'est la
qualité de la fièvre qu'on se donne pour le faire. Puis,
qu'est-ce que fait une répétition ou une négligence de
syntaxe, si la création est neuve, si la conception est
originale, s'il y a, ici et là, une épithète ou un tour de
phrase, qui vaille en lui seul cent pages d'une prose
impeccable, qualité ordinaire?

Id.

Apollon à portes ouvertes
Laisse indifféremment cueillir
Les belles feuilles toujours vertes
Qui gardent les noms de vieillir:
Mais l'art d'en faire des couronnes
N'est pas su de toutes personnes;
Et trois ou quatre seulement,
Au monde desquels on me range,
Peuvent donner une louange
Qui demeure éternellement.

Malherbe.

This bears out Don Quixote's opinion of poets:

"There does not exist a poet", he said, "who is not arrogant and does not think that he is the greatest poet in the world."

"There is no rule without exception," answered Don Lorenzo, "and there is such a thing as a poet who is great but who does not think so."

"Few", answered Don Quixote.

(*Pocos, respondió Don Quijote.*)

Here are two more examples of Malherbe's verse:

Tout le plaisir des jours est en leurs matinées:
La nuit est déjà proche à qui passe midi.

La moisson de nos champs lassera les faucilles,
Et les fruits passeront la promesse des fleurs.

These examples which I have quoted have all of them a beauty of outline, a classic limpidity and simplicity, which make one feel that Malherbe was not unjustified in having so high an opinion of his own work. It is interesting to compare it, not with the work of the Renaissance which he set out to destroy, or with that of the Romantics which would have shocked him still more, but with a poet who was also a classical artist, André Chénier; with this, for instance:

Et sur ses blonds cheveux, en couronne brillante,
Mêler la rose blanche et la rose sanglante,
Que les dieux du Liban virent naître jadis
Des larmes de Vénus et du sang d'Adonis.

[270]

or this:

> C'est le dieu de Nysa, c'est le vainqueur du Gange,
> Au visage de vierge, au front ceint de vendange.

These last lines remind one of Keats, and especially of his description of Bacchus in the last canto of *Endymion*:

> 'Twas Bacchus and his kin!
> Like to a moving vintage down they came,
> Crown'd with green leaves, and faces all on flame.

Side by side with the fragments from Malherbe there are some fragments of Ronsard, the prince of poets, whose work Malherbe considered he had successfully annihilated. He forgot, however, the whirligig of time.

These are two separate poems on Mary Queen of Scots:

> *Au milieu du Printemps entre les Liz nasquit*
> *Son corps, qui de blancheur les Liz mesmes veinquit,*
> *Et les Roses qui sont du sang d'Adonis teintes,*
> *Furent par sa couleur de leur vermeil dépeintes:*

> In middle spring between the lilies born,
> Her body whiter than the lilies gleamed,
> And roses from Adonis' blood were shorn
> Of their live colour, and less roses seemed.

> *Ainsi qu'on voit demy-blanche et vermeille*
> *Naistre l'Aurore, et Vesper sur la nuit,*
> *Ainsi sur toute en beauté nompareille*
> *Des Escossois la Princesse reluit.*

> Just as we see, half rosy and half white,
> Dawn and the morning star dispel the night,
> In beauty thus beyond compare impearled,
> The Queen of Scotland rises on the world.

Here is a passage from a sonnet:

> *Ces longues nuicts d'hyver, où la Lune ocieuse*
> *Tourne si lentement son char tout à l'entour,*
> *Où le Coq si tardif nous annonce le jour,*
> *Où la nuict semble un an à l'âme soucieuse.*

[271]

Those long-protracted nights of winter slumber-bound,
When the slow moon so still her chariot drives around,
When the Dawn so delays to answer Chanticleer,
And the dark nights do seem to watchful soul a year.

I made these translations for a book, but the first one has been translated by Swinburne, and will be found in his play *Chastelard*. My two favourite lines of Ronsard are:

> La Parque t'a tuée et cendre tu reposes,

and, from *The Hymn to Death*:

> Je te salue, heureuse et profitable mort!

The first has the grace of a Greek epigram, the second is like the call of a silver trumpet.

People come and make a hole in you. When it's animals, it's not their fault, but human beings needn't. They make a hole, and they go away and leave it.

R. C. Hutchinson.

To be a musician is to fight every day of your life.

Nathan.

Something strong and genial, and immeasurably kind, had gone out of the world, leaving it too much the poorer for thought to endure.

Alexander Laing.

Tous les grands poètes, sans aucune exception, si ce n'est au dix-neuvième siècle, ont été réactionnaires comme on dit, également ennemis des tribuns et des pédants. C'est un fait, et on n'y peut rien. Les textes sont là, d'Homère à Baudelaire, de la Genèse à Goethe, d'Aristophane à Cervantes et d'Eschyle à Shakespeare.

André Suarès.

I copied this out of a French newspaper when I was at Rome in 1934. It was written *à propos* of *Coriolanus*, which had just been performed at the Théâtre Français in Paris and had been stopped by the Government because it was too "actual" and excited too greatly the passions of the audience.

M. Suarès might have proved the rule by giving Milton as the exception.

I heard great Hector sounding war's alarms,
Where thro' the listless ghosts chiding he strode.

They say Achilles in the darkness stirred
And...Hector, his old enemy,
Moved the great shades that were his limbs. They heard
More than Olympian thunder on the sea.

Still as the sea, ere winds were taught to blow,
Or moving spirit bade the waters flow;
Still as the slumber of a saint forgiv'n,
And mild as op'ning gleams of promis'd heav'n.

Then conscience sleeps and leaving nature free,
All my loose soul unbounded springs to thee.

I have often shown these quotations to people who were not able to trace them; especially the first and the second. I leave the reader the fun of guessing who the authors are.

*Il y a une grâce, une cadence, une majesté de la phrase
que l'écrivain soucieux de gloire emprunte au goût de
l'époque. C'est par là qu'il vieillit. Le style qui a résonné
avec trop de charme s'éteint. Le temps conserve de
préférence ce qui est un peu sec.*
J. Chardonne.

There is a grace, a cadence, a majesty of phrase which
the writer who is careful of fame borrows from the taste
of his time. It is that part of his work which becomes
old-fashioned. The style which has sounded with too
great a charm fades away. Time prefers to preserve what
is a little bit dry.

 This explains why the style of Stendhal's *Chartreuse de Parme*
and *Le Rouge et le Noir*, the style of Mérimée's best stories, of
Jane Austen's novels and Thackeray's *Esmond*, does not now
seem a day more old-fashioned than when these authors were
writing. Writers, on the other hand, whose style had an enormous
vogue for more than one generation, such as Byron and Moore,
Rossetti, Swinburne and Pater, and Pierre Loti, seem old-
fashioned except at those moments when they attain, either
through baldness or felicity, to that simplicity which is common
to all great poetry and which is ageless. It would be a mistake
to think that this never happens even to a writer so exotic as
Rossetti or so sumptuous as Swinburne; for instance, take
Swinburne's

> They gave him light in his ways,
> And love, and a space for delight,
> And beauty and length of days,
> And night, and sleep in the night.

Or take Rossetti's

> How large that thrush looks on the bare thorn-tree!

(an instance of baldness), or his

>   and there be they
> Who kissed his wings which brought him yesterday
> And thank his wings to-day that he is flown

[278]

(an instance of felicity of which any of the Elizabethans might have been proud).

Thackeray's style had enough charm to please his contemporaries, and enough dryness to remain fresh in the store-cupboard of time. Andrew Lang quotes as one of his most beautiful sentences this short passage from *The Newcomes*:

> And the past and its dear histories, and youth and its hopes and passions, and tones and looks, for ever echoing in the heart, and present in the memory. Those, no doubt, poor Clive saw and heard as he looked across the great gulf of time and parting and grief, and beheld the woman he had loved for many years.

One of my favourite sentences of his is this:

> I felt as one who had been walking below the sea, and treading amidst the bones of shipwrecks.

"Bones" is the operative word.

Here is an example of grave prose, like the mellow tones of a beautifully played 'cello. It is from Belloc's *Hills and the Sea*, in an essay called *The Fall of the Leaf*, which is beautiful from beginning to end, solemn, melancholy, and majestic. I should like to quote it all. Writing of the fall of the leaf, he says:

> With what a pageantry of every sort is not that troubling symbol surrounded! The scent of life is never fuller in the woods than now, for the ground is yielding up its memories. The spring when it comes will not restore this fulness, nor these deep and ample recollections of the earth. For the earth seems now to remember the drive of the ploughshare and its harrying; the seed, and the full bursting of it, the swelling and the completion of the harvest. Up to the edge of the woods throughout the weald the earth has borne fruit; the barns are full, and the wheat is standing stacked in the fields; and there are orchards all around. It is upon such a mood of parentage and of fruition that the leaves fall.

[279]

As a prose writer he has other chords to his lyre: wit, irony, vividness, gusto, and, above all, vision. Here is an example of that:

> So perished the French Monarchy. Its dim origins stretched out and lost themselves in Rome; it had already learnt to speak and recognized its own nature when the vaults of the Thermae echoed heavily to the slow footsteps of the Merovingian kings. Look up that vast valley of dead men crowned, and you may see the gigantic figure of Charlemagne, his brows level and his long white beard tangled like an undergrowth, having in his left hand the globe and in his right the hilt of an unconquerable sword. There also are the short, strong horsemen of the Robertian house, half-hidden by their leather shields, and their sons before them growing in vestment and majesty, and taking on the pomp of the Middle Ages. Louis VII, all covered with iron; Philip the Conqueror; Louis IX, who alone is surrounded with light; they stand in a widening, interminable procession, this great crowd of kings; they lose their armour, they take their ermine on, they are accompanied by their captains and their marshals; at last, in their attitude and in their magnificence, they sum up in themselves the pride and the achievement of the French nation. But time has dissipated what it could not tarnish, and the process of a thousand years has turned these mighty figures into unsubstantial things. You may see them in the grey end of darkness, like a pageant all standing still. You look again, but with the growing light and with the wind that rises before morning they have disappeared.

Here is an example of the perfection of effortless ease in prose, from an article written by E. V. Lucas called *Paris Revisited*:

> Although "February fill-dyke" is a familiar phrase—made more familiar by Millais's great wet landscape—the second month in the year has a habit of giving us one or two days, windless and cloudless, and of a tender lucidity; days which are like promissory notes issued by spring and

certain to be honoured. The February that has just passed gave us not one or two, but a full dozen, and three of these I spent in Paris, observing again how that city, though only seven hours distant from London by rail and steamer, and half that by air, is ahead of us in temperature; so that where I had left merely thickening twigs I found buds, and where I had left buds I found leaves. As for the Parisians, they had made up their minds that this interlude was not a foretaste of spring, but the genuine article, with the result that when I made my way to Auteuil to lunch first and see some steeplechasing after, I found a Bois filled with picnic parties: the grassy spaces lively with children at play and the water crowded with boats; while the more reposeful and careless folk lay about as though it were midsummer, and no such calamity as rheumatism had been invented.

I am an old and solitary man,
Mine eyes feel dimly out the setting sun,
Which drops its great red fruit of bitterness
To-day as other days, as every day,
Within the patient waters

Browning.

I came across these lines quoted in a newspaper, forgot or
never knew whom they were by, and tried to trace them for
many years in vain. I consulted many experts, saying I thought
they were by Browning. Rudyard Kipling told me he thought
the second line sounded like Browning, but he had no idea by
whom they were written, and that he had searched through
Browning in vain. Then one day in a bookshop I found the lines
in a posthumous poem of Browning's called *Soliloquy of
Aeschylus* in the complete collected edition in one volume.

I was asked to translate the first stanza of the following very well-known poem by Pushkin:

Я пережилъ свои желанья,
Я разлюбилъ свои мечты;
Остались мнѣ одни страданья,
Плоды сердечной пустоты.

Подъ бурями судьбы жестокой
Увялъ цвѣтущій мой вѣнецъ!
Живу печальный, одинокій,
И жду: придетъ ли мой конецъ?

Такъ, позднимъ хладомъ пораженный,
Какъ бури слышенъ зимній свистъ,
Одинъ на вѣткѣ обнаженной
Трепещетъ запоздалый листъ.

I made an attempt at the whole poem; here it is:

I've lived to bury my desires
And see my dreams corrode with rust;
Now all that's left are fruitless fires
That burn my empty heart to dust.

Struck by the storms of cruel fate
My crown of summer bloom is sere;
Alone and sad I watch and wait
And wonder if the end is near,

As conquered by the last cold air
When winter whistles in the wind,
Alone upon a bough that's bare,
A trembling leaf is left behind.

This reminds me of four lines of Pascoli, from a poem called *Il Nido* (The Nest):

> *Or v' è sola una piuma, che all' invito*
> *Del vento esita, palpita leggera:*
> *Qual sogno antico in anima severa*
> *Fuggente sempre e non ancor fuggito.*

Now there's one feather which by breezes bidden
Is wavering and trembling frail and light,
As in a soul austere a dream stays hidden,
About to fly, but not yet taking flight.

Notre ignorance de l'histoire nous fait calomnier notre temps. On a toujours été comme ça.

Gustave Flaubert.

Le vrai bon théâtre, c'est une émotion ou une gaîté procurée n'importe comment.

Edmond de Goncourt.

I have always thought that all theories of what a good play is, or how a good play should be written, are futile. A good play is a play which when acted upon the boards makes an audience interested and pleased. A play that fails in this is a bad play.

Que l'heure est donc brève
Qu'on passe en aimant!
C'est moins qu'un moment,
Un peu plus qu'un rêve.
Le temps nous enlève
Notre enchantement.

These lines occur in Alphonse Daudet's novel, *Le Nabab*. Not long before he died, Mr Broadbent sent me a translation of these lines into the following Latin couplet:

Quam breve tempus abit quod amando degitur! instar
momenti fugiens somnia vix superat.

He asked me to trace the authorship of the French. I tried, but without success. The lines must have been set to music, and sung in drawing-rooms.

Since the book was published the quotation was traced for me by the kindness of an American correspondent.

The lines were written by Armand Silvestre, who died in 1901. They were set to music by Massenet. There is a second stanza:

Que l'heure est donc brève,
Qu'on passe en aimant!
En aimant!
Sous le flot dormant
Soupirait la grève;
M'aimas-tu vraiment?
Fut-ce seulement
Un peu plus qu'un rêve?
Que l'heure est donc brève,
Qu'on passe en aimant!
En aimant!

His Eyes were languishing, and yet had a peculiar sort of lustre: his Hair was curled, and yellow, resembling Flame, when he walked in the sun; which made some men fancy he was powdered with dust of Gold.

Herodian, Translated by a Gentleman of Oxford, 1698.

The great artists are all contemporaries.

Progress in art is progress towards simplicity.

Lionel Johnson.

Lionel Johnson said that Hardy's was "a mind enamoured of meditation but impatient of dreams".

About Hardy and Wordsworth he wrote:

> And when either indulges his genius in all its strength and beauty, he gives voice to the very earth under his feet.

This is true of Wordsworth when he writes lines such as:

> Upon the margin of that moorish flood
> Motionless as a cloud the old Man stood,
> That heareth not the loud winds when they call:
> And moveth all together, if it move at all.

Or these:

> And in the meadows and the lower grounds
> Was all the sweetness of a common dawn.

Or these:

> About the fields I wander, knowing this
> Only, that what I seek I cannot find.

Thine eyes shall see the King in His beauty. They shall behold a land of far distances.

Isaiah.

Cares make peevish: mine
Weigh me (but 'tis a secret) to my grave.

Night has its first, supreme, forsaken star.

Browning.

Gowing is sometimes very tedious with his remarks, and
not always cautious; and Carrie once very properly
reminded him that she was present.

Grossmith, *Diary of a Nobody*.

"Let us never be blind", said Mr Pumblechook, "to her faults of temper, but it is to be hoped she meant well."

Dickens, *Great Expectations.*

The word amateur has come by the thousand oddities of language to convey an idea of tepidity; whereas the word itself has the meaning of passion. Nor is this peculiarity confined to the mere form of the word; the actual characteristic of these nameless dilettanti is a genuine fire and reality. A man must love a thing very much if he not only practises it without any hope of fame or money, but even practises it without any hope of doing it well. Such a man must love the toils of the work more than any other man can love the rewards of it.

G. K. Chesterton.

I shall keep your honour safe;
With mine I trust you, as the sculptor trusts
Yon marble woman with the marble rose,
Loose on her hand she never will let fall,
In graceful, slight, silent security.

Browning, *Colombe's Birthday*.

There's light—
Light all about me, and I move to it.
Browning, *A Blot on the Scutcheon*.

He lightly skirmishes on every string
Charg'd with a flying touch.

How a pure spirit should incarnate be,
And Life, itself, wear Death's frail livery.

Crashaw.

Les grands artistes sont des êtres, qui suivant le mot de Napoléon, interceptent à volonté la communication que la nature a mise entre les sens et la pensée. Molière et Talma, dans leur vieillesse, ont été plus amoureux que ne le sont les hommes ordinaires.

Balzac, Une Fille d'Ève.

L'admiration est toujours une fatigue pour l'espèce humaine.

Le Bal de Sceaux.

Les artistes gênés sont impitoyables ; ils fuient ou se moquent.

La Maison du Chat qui Pelote.

Artists when they are bored are merciless: they either laugh at you or go away.

Il n'y a que le génie qui sache se renouveler comme le serpent.

Modeste Mignon.

The ability to weigh two duties, and balance them against each other, is the measure of human worth and dignity. It rings through the *Antigone* of Sophocles as it does through the *Apology* of Socrates, and nowhere will it be found more clearly than in More's writings in prison. It was as one of a mighty company that, on Thursday, 6 July, 1535, he spoke on the scaffold his last words: that they should pray for him in this world, and he would pray for them elsewhere, protesting that he died the King's good servant, but God's first.

R. W. Chambers, *Life of Sir Thomas More.*

The two finest poems about death that I know, in modern languages, were written by a Spaniard and a Russian. The Spanish poem expresses an agnostic view, the Russian, as would be expected, the sentiments of a Christian. The Spaniard's is by Don Gustavo A. Becquer: it is too long to quote.

The Russian poem is by Count Alexis Tolstoi. It is called *Tropar*, in imitation of the ἰδιόμελα of St John Damascene. It was a part of the funeral service of the Eastern Church, blent with other motifs in the same service.

Какая сладость въ жизни сей
Земной печали не причастна?
Чье ожиданье не напрасно.
И гдѣ счастливый межъ людей?
Все то превратно, все ничтожно,
Что́ мы съ трудомъ пріобрѣли —
Какая слава на земли
Стоитъ тверда и непреложна?
Все пепелъ, призракъ, тѣнь и дымъ,
Исчезнетъ все, какъ вихорь пыльный
И передъ смертыю мы стоимъ
И безоружны и безсильны.
Рука могучаго слаба,
Ничтожны царскія велѣнья —
Прійми усопшаго раба,
Господь, въ блаженныя селенья!

Какъ ярый витязь смерть нашла
Меня, какъ хищникъ низложила,
Свой зѣвъ разинула могила
И все житейское взяла.
Спасайтесь, сродники и чада,
Изъ гроба къ вамъ взываю я.
Спасайтесь, братья и друзья,
Да не узрите пламень ада!
Вся жизнь есть царство суеты,
И, дуновенье смерти чуя,
Мы увядаемъ какъ цвѣты —

Почто же мы мятемся всуе?
Престолы наши суть гроба,
Чертоги наши разрушенье—
Пріими усопшаго раба,
Господь, въ блаженныя селенья!

Средь груды тлѣющихъ костей
Кто царь, кто рабъ, судья иль воинъ
Кто царства Божія достоинъ,
И кто отверженный злодѣй?
О, братья, гдѣ сребро и злато,
Гдѣ сонмы многіе рабовъ?
Среди невѣдомыхъ гробовъ
Кто есть убогій, кто богатый?
Все пепелъ, дымъ, и пыль, и прахъ,
Все призракъ, тѣнь и привидѣнье—
Лишь х Тебя, на небесахъ,
Господь, и пристань и спасенье!
Исчезнетъ все, что было плоть,
Величье наше будетъ тлѣнье—
Пріими усопшаго, Господь,
Въ Твои блаженныя селенья!

И Ты, предстательница всѣмъ,
И Ты, заступница скорбящимъ,
Къ Тебѣ о братѣ, здѣсь лежащемъ,
Къ Тебѣ, Святая, вопіемъ!
Моли божественного Сына,
Его, Пречистая, моли,
Дабы отжившій на земли
Оставилъ здѣсь свои кручины!
Все пепелъ, прахъ, и дымъ, и тѣнь,
О, други, призраку не вѣрьте!
Когда дохнетъ въ нежданный день
Дыханье тлительное смерти,
Мы всѣ поляжемъ какъ хлѣба,

Серпомъ подрѣзанные въ нивахъ —
Пріими усопшаго раба,
Господь, въ селеніяхъ счастливыхъ!

Иду въ незнаемый я путь,
Иду межъ страха и надежды;
Мой взоръ угасъ, остыла грудь,
Не внемлеть слухъ, сомкнуты вѣжды;
Лежу безгласенъ, недвижимъ,
Не слышу братскаго рыданья,
И отъ кадила синій дымъ
Не мнѣ струить благоуханье:
Но вѣчнымъ сномъ пока я сплю,
Моя любовь не умираетъ,
И ею, братья, васъ молю,
Да каждый къ Господу взываетъ:
Господь! Въ тотъ день, когда труба
Вострубитъ міра преставленье —
Пріими усопшаго раба
Въ Твои блаженныя селенья!

What joy does this life possess that is not mingled with earthly sorrow? What hope is not in vain and where among mortals is there one who is happy? Of all the fruits of our labour and toil there is nothing which shall endure nor anything of any value. Where is the earthly glory that shall abide and pass not away? All things are but ashes, phantom, shadow, and smoke. Everything shall vanish as the dust of a whirlwind; and face to face with death we are unarmed and without defence; the right hand of the mighty is feeble and the commands of kings are as nothing. Receive, O Lord, Thy departed Servant into Thy happy dwelling-place!

Death, like a furious knight-at-arms, encountered me, and like a robber he hath laid me low; the grave hath opened its jaws and hath taken away from me all that was alive. Save yourselves, kinsmen and children. I call to you from the grave. Be saved, O my brothers, O my

[303]

friends, so that you behold not the flames of hell! Life is a kingdom of vanity, and as we breathe the corruption of death, we wither away like flowers. Why do we toss about in vain? Our thrones are nothing but graves and our palaces but ruins. Receive, O Lord, Thy departed Servant into Thy happy dwelling-place!

Amidst the heap of rotting bones, who is king or servant or judge or warrior? Who shall deserve the Kingdom of God, and who shall be the outcast and the evil-doer? O brothers, where is the gold and the silver, where are the hosts of servants? Among the forgotten graves who is the rich man and who is the poor man? All is but ashes and smoke, and dust and mould, phantom and shadow and dream; only with Thee in Heaven, O Lord, is there refuge and salvation; all that was once flesh shall disappear and our pomps shall fall into decay. Receive, O Lord, Thy departed Servant into Thy happy dwelling-place!

And Thou who dost intercede on behalf of us all, Thou the defender of the oppressed: to Thee, most blessed among women, we cry on behalf of our brother who lies here. Pray to Thy Divine Son, pray, O most Immaculate, for him: that having fulfilled his life upon earth, he may leave his sorrow behind him. All things are but ashes, dust and smoke and shadow. O friends, put not your faith in a phantom! When, on some sudden day, the corruption of death shall breathe upon us, we shall perish like wheat, mown down by the sickle in the corn-fields. Receive, O Lord, Thy departed Servant into Thy happy dwelling-place!

I follow I know not what path; half in hope and half in fear I go; my sight is dimmed, my heart has grown chill, my hearing is faint, my eyelids are closed; I am lying voiceless and I cannot move, I cannot hear the wailing of the brethren, and the blue smoke from the censer brings to me no fragrance; yet, until I sleep the eternal sleep, my love shall not die, and in the name of that love I implore you, O my brothers, that each one of you may thus call upon God: "Lord, on that day, when the trumpet shall sound the end of the world, receive Thy departed Servant into Thy happy dwelling-place!"

Ce que je sais de Dieu? Exactement ce qu'en dit le catéchisme: ni plus, ni moins.

P. Claudel.

Je n'ai plus que faire céans, puisque ma dame m'envoie au loin préparer la maison claire que je lui ai promise, la maison de cristal, fleurie de roses, lumineuse au matin quand reluit le soleil!

Joseph Bédier, *Le Roman de Tristan et Iseult.*

Peace, gentlemen, I go and will not stay. My Lady sends me to prepare that shining home I vowed her, of crystal, and of rose shot through with morning.

Belloc.

And therefore, lady, sithen ye have taken you to perfection, I must neede take me to perfection of right. For
I take record of God, in you I have had mine earthly joy.

Malory, Morte d'Arthur.

" Ponite" inquit "hoc corpus ubicunque: nihil vos ejus cura conturbet; tantum illud vos rogo, ut ad domini altare memineritis, ubi fueritis."

St Augustine.

Ah, could thy grave at home, at Carthage, be!
Care not for that, and lay me where I fall!
Everywhere heard will be the judgment-call;
But at God's altar, oh! remember me.

Matthew Arnold.

Τίς ξένος, ὦ ναυηγέ; Λεόντιχος ἐνθάδε νεκρὸν
εὗρεν ἐπ' αἰγιαλούς, χῶσε δὲ τῷδε τάφῳ
Δακρύσας ἐπίκηρον ἑὸν βίον· οὐδὲ γὰρ αὐτὸς
ἥσυχος, αἰθυίῃ δ' ἴσα θαλασσοπορεῖ.

Callimachus.

Who are you, shipwrecked man? Leontichus found
My corpse on the shore and over it heaped this mound,
Bewailing his own sad life, for neither is he
At peace, but flits like a sea-gull over the sea.

Et à l'heure de ma mort soyez le refuge de mon âme
étonnée et recevez-la dans le sein de votre miséricorde.

St Margaret Mary.

And at the hour of my death harbour my awestruck
soul and receive me into the heart of Thy mercy.

L

INDEX

ACHILLES, his mother's moving speech to, 17; would rather be a live dog on earth than King of the Ghosts, 18; his might, 29; talks to his horse Xanthus, 34; kills Lycaon, 35; slays Hector, 36, 37; his grief for Patroclus, 37; his sadness, 39; touched by Priam's grief, 41

AENEAS, on beholding the shade of Marcellus, 29

AESCHYLUS, on the ubiquity of affliction, 53; quotations from, 54, 55

ALBERT, the Emperor, 100, 101

ALCINOUS, KING, his tribute to Ulysses, 10

AMATEUR, G. K. CHESTERTON on the, 295

ANSTEY, his talking horse, 34

ARNOLD, MATTHEW, his contempt of Pope, 21; his *Sohrab and Rustum*, 27; on Dante, 105; translation of St Augustine, 309

ART, weaker than necessity, 54; the progress of, 289

ARTIST, definition of an, 106

ASQUITH, enjoyed George Eliot, 121

ATLAS, his misery, 82

AUGUSTINE, ST, quotation from, 309

AUSTEN, JANE, her style, 278

BALIUS, the horse of Achilles, 34

BALZAC, his powerful vision, 215; on artists, admiration, and genius, 299

BARING, T. C., attempted to translate Horace, 66

BAUDELAIRE, an excellent poet, 183, 184

BEACONSFIELD, LORD, preferred a new book to a classic, 3; quotations from, 155

BEAUMARCHAIS, 181

BEAUTY, the bane of the beautiful, 48

BECQUER, DON GUSTAVO, his fine poem on death, 301

BEETHOVEN, his deafness, 6; achieved tragedy and peace, 26; his sadness, 33; 136; death of, 172

[313]

CALVUS, Father Ronald Knox's pastiche of, 90

CANNING, attempted to translate Horace, 66

CANOVA, his bust of Helen, 268

CATULLUS, an Air by, 137; his magical melody, 27, 28; the
    tenderest of Roman poets, 76; his lines on the death of
    Quintilia, 76; his elegy on the death of his brother, 77, 78;
    on farewell to love, 79, 80; his lyrics, 80

CERVANTES, a soldier and adventurer, 145

CHAPMAN, influence of his Homer on Keats, 89

CHARDONNE, Jacques, quotations from, 267

CHATEAUBRIAND, his fine writing, 216; one of Napoleon's
    remarks recorded by, 217; his remark about Talleyrand as
    a prophet, 218; bewailed the infidelity of his time, 218

CHAUCER, his imitations of Dante, 107, 108; a diplomatist, 145

CHEHOV, all his plays symbolic, 175

CHÉNIER, André, quotations from, 270, 271

CHESTERTON, G. K., quotation from, 227; on the Catholic
    Church, 230; on literature, 255; on the amateur, 295

CHRISTIAN FAITH, cannot be written about from the outside,
    147

CHURCH, the differences between the Anglican and the
    Catholic, 177; the Catholic, 230–233

CHURCH, A. J., his *Stories from Homer*, 31

CIMABUE, ousted by Giotto, 3

COLERIDGE, his sentence on snow, 206

COMMUNISTS, their view of marriage, 5

CONSTANT, Benjamin, on man's need of religion, 237

CONTRADICTION, Tolstoi's advice about, 253

CORNEILLE, his dislike of Racine's *Britannicus*, 167; his great-
    ness, 220

CORNEY GRAIN, his entertainments, 234, 235

CORNISH, F. W., his admiration of George Eliot, 121

COURT-MARTIAL, Dr Johnson's view of a certain, 120

COWLEY, a literary curiosity, 86; wrote one fine elegy, 87

COWPER, his successful translation of a famous ode by
    Horace, 68, 69

CRABBE, his use of the heroic couplet, 22; his descriptions of
    landscape, 207

CRASHAW, quotation from, 298
CROCUSES, 240

D'ANNUNZIO, quotations from, 143
DANTE, on the swift revolutions of fashion in literature, 3; inferior to Homer, 15; his sadness, 33; his description of Paolo and Francesca, 95–97; his lines on the Southern Cross, 98, 99; on the dawn, 99; his magical touch in describing landscape, 100; his apostrophe to Italy, 100, 101; 102; his vision of Matilda, 103; his vision of Beatrice, 103, 104; his description of blossom, 104; 105; on exile, 106; the greatest artist who ever lived, 106; his St Bernard's Hymn to our Lady, 106, 107; Shakespeare may have read, 109; was intimately linked with human activities, 145
DEATH, the peace of, 11; grief at a friend's, 12; the unending toll of, 23; Mrs BREWSTER's lines on, 112, 113; RONSARD's *Hymn to*, 272; TOLSTOI's poem on, 301–303; prayer at the hour of, 310
DEBUSSY, death of, 172
DEIPHOBUS, deserts Hector, 36
DESTINY, JOHN OLIVER HOBBES' definition of, 252
DEVELOPMENT, the period of, the most interesting in a man's life, 174
DICKENS, his powerful vision, 215; quotation from, 294
DISOBEDIENCE, R. A. WASON on, 225
DONNE, would have been regarded as greater had he written less, 110; 111
DON QUIXOTE, his opinion of actors, 194; quotations from, 194–196, 204; his opinion of poets, 270
DOSTOIEVSKI, a disciple of Victor Hugo, 137; a fine prose writer, 218
DREYFUS CASE, the, 120
DRYDEN, attempted to translate Horace, 66; his translation of Virgil's lines to Marcellus, 71; and of his exquisite picture of Italian cities, 73; and of some lines from the *Georgics*, 75; 181
DUSE, 190

[316]

GRAY, his fragment of a poem in Latin, 89; a Dante scholar, 100; some lines rejected from his *Elegy*, 187

GREEK LANGUAGE, the superiority of the, 15; the pronunciation of the, 142, 143

GREEKS, the, their view of the world of shades, 18

GRIMM, his *Goose Girl*, 34

GROSSMITH, quotation from, 293

GUEST, speeding the parting, 13

HALS, FRANZ, superior to some modern artists, 123

HARDY, the nature of his mind, 290

HARRISON, CLIFFORD, his recitations, 121, 122

HECTOR, his infant son, 24; his nobility, 29; death of, 36; Priam begs Achilles for his body, 40, 41

HEINE, his lyrics, 80; on the misery of Atlas, 82; on the sorrowing lover, 83; his poem on the harlot and the thief, 83, 84; 146; on the stupidity of the heartless, 166; his conflicts produced results, 174

HELEN, of Troy, her beauty made the Trojan War worth while, 20

HEREDIA, possessed an Horatian perfection of phase, 69

HERODIAN, quotation from, 288

HERZEN, Russian Socialist reformer, 116

HOBBES, JOHN OLIVER, quotations from, 201–203, 252

HOGARTH, superior to certain modern artists, 123

HOMER, on the swift revolutions of fashion in literature, 3; praises happy marriage, 5; his blindness, 6; his lines on sorrow, 7; his description of Elpenor's death, 8; on the peace of death, 11; on grief at a friend's death, 12; on speeding the parting guest, 13; regarded war as an unmixed evil, 20; his perfect description of Helen, 20; POPE'S translation of, the best, 20; his deep melancholy, 23; his tender pictures of womanhood and children, 24; achieves tragedy and peace, 26; his simile of the poppy, 27; on the glory of the young, 29; his immense sadness, 33; on the amateur, 42

HOOD, THOMAS, his translation of Horace's Ode to Pyrrha, 66

[319]

MALHERBE, quotations from, 270

MALLOCK, W. H., on Catholicism, 231, 232

MALORY, quotations from his *Morte d'Arthur*, 308

MARCELLUS, VIRGIL's description of, 29; and his famous lines to, 71

MARLOWE, inspired by Ovid, 88; passages from the *Jew of Malta*, 131, 132; and Shakespeare compared, 132, 164, 165; regarded as author of *Richard III*, 129

MARRIAGE, HOMER praises happy, 5; the Communists' view of, 5; a mother's curious idea of a good marriage for her daughter, 226; GOETHE on, 258

MARSH, EDWARD, translation of Aeschylus, 55; of Lucretius, 58; of La Fontaine, 152, 153

MARTINDALE, FATHER C. C., quotation from, 248

MAUPASSANT, reminiscent of Tacitus, 93; neglected in France, 123; his descriptions of landscape, 206

MEREDITH, GEORGE, his popularity confined to intellectuals, 121; will be rediscovered, 265

MÉRIMÉE, his style, 278

MEYNELL, MRS, her admiration of Swinburne, 87

MILTON, his blindness, 6; attempted to translate Horace, 66; wrote *Paradise Lost* in a kind of Latin-English, 66; 73; possibly inspired by Tacitus, 94; 101, 139, 143; a civil servant, 145; on freedom, 154; three fragments from, 222

MINCIUS, Milton's "smooth-sliding", 73

MOLIÈRE, an actor, 145; his *Tartuffe* and *Le Misanthrope* symbolic, 175; 181; quotations from his *Psyché*, 241

MOORE, his style, 278

MORE, SIR THOMAS, his imprisonment and death, 300

MOZART, died at 36, 178; 182

MUSICIAN, the hard life of a, 274

MUSSET, ALFRED DE, faints on hearing Rachel recite Racine, 115; 146, 148; his love story, 260

MYERS, FREDERICK, on Homer's greatness and the superiority of the Greek language, 15, 16; his translation of some famous lines by Virgil, 70–72; on Lucretius, 79; on Virgil, 88, 89

[321]

[322]

SHAKESPEARE, had little Greek, 2; on speeding the parting guest, 13; his language barbarous compared with Homer, 15; his sadness, 33; his sonnets reminiscent of Catullus, 76; inspired by Ovid, 88; 101; may have read Dante, 109; passage from his *Richard III*, 129–131; and Marlowe compared, 132, 164; 139; an actor, 145; his description of the dawn, 184; controversy about what he meant by "estridges", 210–214; 266

SHAW-STEWART, PATRICK, poem by, 39

SHELLEY, his beautiful translation of part of Virgil's xth *Eclogue*, 74; his copious flow, 89; 133; VERNON LEE on, 173; 184; passages from, 185, 186; greater than Keats, 186

SIMONIDES, on a period of calm in winter, 56

SITWELL, EDITH, her admiration of Pope, 22

SKELTON, religious poem by, 199, 200

SOLESMES, the Abbot of, at the tomb of the Scipios, 188

SOPHOCLES, declared men were shadows, 47

SORROW, the value of, 7

SOUL, the human, ANDRÉ MAUROIS on, 250

STENDHAL, his *Le Rouge et le Noir*, 9; his style, 278

STEVENSON, R. L., his description of J. A. Symonds' conversation, 119; his description of the dawn, 264

STRACHEY, LYTTON, his admiration of Pope, 22

STYLE, simplicity makes it ageless, 278

SWINBURNE, his *Ave Atque Vale* to Baudelaire, 85, 86; EDMUND GOSSE's opinion of, 86; was never regarded as a minor poet, 87; his translation of the *Dies Irae*, 91, 92; his admiration of Victor Hugo, 137; 141, 272; his style, 278

SYMONDS, JOHN ADDINGTON, description of his conversation by R. L. STEVENSON, 119

TACITUS, his description of Poppaea, 92, 93; his biting irony, 93, 94

TALLEYRAND, a prophet, 218; his description of his mother, 256

TASSO, a Russian's opinion of, 181; 182

[324]

TENNYSON, his paraphrase of some lines by Lucretius, 59; a
fine painter of landscape, 207, 208, 209
TERRY, ELLEN, on realism following after the idea, 234
THACKERAY, on the inscription round the dome of the
Temple, 176; his style, 278, 279
THEODORA, EMPRESS, 57
THETIS, her moving speech to Achilles, 17; goes to Olympus
in spite of her sorrow, 38; her grief, 39
TITUS, his love for Berenice, 115
TOLSTOI, the excellent beginning of his *Anna Karenina*, 195; a
fine prose writer, 218; quotations from, 253; on *Anna
Karenina*, 263
TRISTAN ET ISEULT, Le Roman de, quotation from, 307
TROLLOPE, ANTHONY, rediscovered, 201
TURGENEV, his *Fathers and Sons*, 26; a fine prose writer,
218

ULYSSES, his wisdom and integrity, 10; recognized by his
old nurse, 14; seduced by the siren, 102

VERDI, his opera disliked by ROSSINI, 167
VERE, SIR STEPHEN DE, translated Horace's Ode to Pyrrha,
67
VERLAINE, on the death of Victor Hugo, 138
VIRGIL, inferior to Homer, 15; 27; his description of Marcellus,
29; spoilt at school for the author, 70; his *Georgics* un-
spoilt for the author, 71; his xth *Eclogue*, 73; beautifully
translated by Shelley, 74; inspired Dante, 88
VOLTAIRE, the easy lucidity of his prose, 218
VOWELS, the special colour of French, 115

WALLACE, EDGAR, 123
WAR, HOMER's view of, 20; its inherent tragedy, 41; chooses
the good, 50
WARD, MRS HUMPHRY, her *Helbeck of Bannisdale*, 147
WEAK, the, no freedom for, 265
WEBSTER, quotations from, 157–159; 164, 168, 169